JAMESTOWN **EDUCATION**

Reading Math

Strategies for English Language Learners

Intermediate

Mc Graw Hill **Glencoe**

New York, New York   Columbus, Ohio   Chicago, Illinois   Peoria, Illinois   Woodland Hills, California

JAMESTOWN EDUCATION

Image Credits: Cover (cube)CORBIS, (calculator)Digital Vision, (globe)Creatas, (others)Getty Images.

 **Glencoe**

Send all inquiries to:
Glencoe/McGraw-Hill
8787 Orion Place
Columbus, OH 43240-4027

ISBN-13: 978-0-07-874228-6 (Student Edition)
ISBN-10: 0-07-874228-5 (Student Edition)
ISBN-13: 978-0-07-874231-6 (Teacher Edition)
ISBN-10: 0-07-874231-5 (Teacher Edition)

Printed in the United States of America.

1 2 3 4 5 6 7 8 9 10 066 11 10 09 08 07 06

Contents

To the Student iv

Pronunciation Key 1

Lessons

1 Athletes' Pay: Men Versus Women 2
2 DeShawn's Paycheck 8
3 The Money Behind the Movies 14
4 The Electoral College 20
5 The Success of Vietnamese Americans 26

Vocabulary Assessment 1–5 32

6 Counting in Native American Beadwork 34
7 Adding and Multiplying are Related 40
8 Worldwide Time Zones 46
9 Statistics 52
10 Newspaper Circulation and Revenue 58

Vocabulary Assessment 6–10 64

11 The Japanese Tatami Measurement 66
12 Discounts and Markups Make a Profit 72
13 Pitching Baseball's Numbers 78
14 How to Count Music in 4/4 Time 84
15 Time to Paint the House 90

Vocabulary Assessment 11–15 96

Glossary 98

Personal Dictionary 101

To the Student

Reading is one of the fastest ways for you to get information. *Reading Math* can help you improve the way you read and understand math topics. You will also learn how to improve your test-taking skills.

Before You Read

These steps can help you *preview* an article and get an idea of what it is about.

Read the title. Ask yourself "What can I learn from the title?" and "What do I already know about this subject?"

Read the first sentence or two. The writer wants to catch your attention in the first sentence or two. You may also find out what you are about to learn.

Skim the entire article. Look over the article quickly for words that may help you understand it. Jot down unfamiliar words in your Personal Dictionary. You can ask someone later what they mean.

Participate in class discussions. Your teacher may show you pictures or objects and ask you questions about them. Try to answer the questions.

While You Read

Here are some tips to help you make sense of what you read:

Concentrate. If your mind wanders, remind yourself of what you learned when you previewed the article.

Ask yourself questions. Ask yourself "What does this mean?" or "How can I use this information?"

Look for the topic of each paragraph. Each paragraph has a main idea. The other sentences build on that idea. Find all of the main ideas to understand the entire article.

Refer to the vocabulary you have learned. The words in dark type will remind you of what you learned in the Vocabulary section. For more help, refer to the previous page.

After You Read

The activities in *Reading Math* will help you practice different ways to learn.

A. Organizing Ideas Webs, charts, and tables will help you organize information from the article. Sometimes you will create art or apply math skills.

B. Comprehension Skills will help you recall facts and understand ideas.

C. Reading Strategies will suggest ways to make sense of what you read.

D. Expanding Vocabulary will teach you more about the vocabulary you learned before and during reading.

Vocabulary Assessment

After every five lessons, you can try out what you have learned. Activities, such as postcards and advertisements, show you how the vocabulary can be useful and fun in everyday life. Enjoy!

Pronunciation Key

a	as in *an* or *cat*	**g**	as in *give, again,* or *dog*
ä	as in *father* or *arm*	**h**	as in *hat, whole,* or *ahead*
ā	as in *made, say,* or *maid*	**j**	as in *jar, enjoy, gentle,* or *badge*
e	as in *wet* or *sell*	**k**	as in *kitchen, book, mock,* or *cool*
ē	as in *he, see, mean, niece,* or *lovely*	**l**	as in *look, alive, heel, tall,* or *follow*
i	as in *in* or *fit*	**m**	as in *me, imagine,* or *seem*
ī	as in *I, mine, sigh, die,* or *my*	**n**	as in *no, inside, inning,* or *fun*
o	as in *on* or *not*	**ng**	as in *singer, bring,* or *drink*
ō	as in *fold, boat, own,* or *foe*	**p**	as in *put, open,* or *drop*
ô	as in *or, oar, naughty, awe,* or *ball*	**r**	as in *run, form,* or *wear*
oo	as in *good, would,* or *put*	**s**	as in *socks, herself,* or *miss*
ōo	as in *roof* or *blue*	**sh**	as in *should, washing,* or *hash*
oi	as in *noise* or *joy*	**t**	as in *too, enter, mitten,* or *sit*
ou	as in *loud* or *now*	**th**	as in *think, nothing,* or *tooth*
u	as in *must* or *cover*	**<u>th</u>**	as in *there, either,* or *smooth*
ū	as in *pure, cue, few,* or *feud*	**v**	as in *vote, even,* or *love*
ur	as in *turn, fern, heard, bird,* or *word*	**w**	as in *well* or *away*
ə	as in *awhile, model, second,* or *column*	**y**	as in *yellow* or *canyon*
b	as in *big, table,* or *job*	**z**	as in *zoo, hazy,* or *sizes*
ch	as in *chew, much,* or *latch*	**zh**	as in *seizure, measure,* or *mirage*
d	as in *deep, puddle,* or *mad*		
f	as in *fat, before, beef, stuff, graph,* or *rough*		

Before You Read

 Think about what you know. Read the lesson title above. What do you think the article may be about? What do you already know about the amounts of money professional athletes earn?

Vocabulary

The content-area and academic English words below appear in "Athletes' Pay: Men Versus Women." Read the definitions and the example sentences.

Content-Area Words

gap (gap) a separation between two things
> *Example:* There is a *gap* of 10 years between my older brother and me.

earnings (ur′ningz) the money a person receives in exchange for work or services
> *Example:* I mowed lawns last summer to increase my *earnings*.

athletes (ath′lēts) people who train for sports and other physical competitions
> *Example:* Swimmers and wrestlers are examples of *athletes*.

salary (sal′ə rē) a set amount of money that a person receives at regular times in exchange for work or services
> *Example:* My father receives his yearly *salary* in 12 monthly paychecks.

market (mär′kit) trade and the exchange of money for a certain service or product
> *Example:* The clothing *market* involves designers who compete for business.

Academic English

professional (prə fesh′ən əl) having a job that is the source of one's income or money
> *Example:* Kayla wants to be a *professional* dancer someday.

contrast (kon′trast) a difference between two things
> *Example:* I felt the *contrast* between the hot air outside and the cool air inside.

Complete the sentences below that contain the content-area and academic English words above. Use the spaces provided. The first one has been done for you.

1. A *professional* cook gets paid to <u>make food</u>.

2. Ana used the *earnings* from her newspaper route to _____.

3. A *market* for a product exists if customers want to _____.

4. There is a *gap* between Mexican culture and _____.

5. I noticed a *contrast* between the tall man and _____.

6. *Athletes* train and practice in order to _____.

7. Chun receives a *salary* in exchange for _____.

 Now skim the article and look for other words that are new to you. Write each new word and its definition in the Personal Dictionary.

While You Read

 Think about why you read. In most professional sports today, women earn less money than men do. Why do you think this is true? As you read, look for the answer.

Athletes' Pay:
Men Versus Women

1   In the United States, women earn 77 cents for each dollar a man earns for the same job. For **professional** athletes, that **gap** is even wider. To get an idea of how wide the gap is, consider the mathematics behind recent figures for **earnings** in professional sports.

5   There were no women on *Forbes Magazine*'s 2004 list of the World's 50 Highest-Paid **Athletes.** The highest-paid athlete on the list was golfer Tiger Woods, who earned $80 million in 2004. In **contrast,** the highest-paid female golfer, Annika Sorenstam, made $5 million. This is about 6 percent of Woods's earnings. The highest-paid woman in sports in 2004 was tennis player Serena

10 Williams, who earned $9.5 million. Her earnings were just 12 percent of Woods's earnings. The top-paid male tennis player, Andre Agassi, made $28 million. This means that Williams made about 34 percent of Agassi's earnings.

    Tennis and golf prize-money amounts also differ for male and female athletes. The average total prize money for a recent five-year period in tennis was $63

15 million for men and $41 million for women. This means that women tennis players' winnings were about 65 percent of men's. The average total prize money for golf was $108.6 million for men and $32.8 million for women. Women golfers' winnings were only about 30 percent of men's. Even so, this prize gap was not as wide as the pay gap between Sorenstam and Woods.

20   Women's and men's professional team sports show an even wider pay gap. For example, in 2003 the Women's National Basketball Association (WNBA) paid its players an average **salary** of $46,000 for the season. The men's NBA paid its players an average of $4.5 million. The pay for women players was about 1 percent of the pay for men.

25   Why is the pay gap between men and women so wide in professional sports? The main reason is the **market.** In many jobs, men and women make the same product or do the same service. However, in professional sports the players themselves are the product. Whether it is fair or not, the money that the players earn is based on crowds and television ratings. Until women's sports attract as

30 many fans as men's sports attract, female athletes will make less money.

    The good news for female athletes is that women's sports are becoming more popular. The WNBA has existed only since 1997, so it is still building its market. It has less than half the amount of teams and games that the NBA has. As the WNBA grows, its players are likely to get paid more money.

LANGUAGE CONNECTION

The noun *earnings* is related to the verb *earn*. *Earnings* means "money that a person earns." What do you think the noun *winnings* means? Try to use it in a sentence.

CONTENT CONNECTION

The Women's Basketball League, or WBL, was the first professional women's basketball league in the United States. The league lasted only from 1978 to 1981. What other professional women's sports do you know about?

After You Read

A. Organizing Ideas

In professional sports, how does the pay for women compare to the pay for men?
Complete the graph below to show the differences between the amounts of money
that male and female athletes earn. Use all of the terms in the box. Mark each amount
on the graph with a line, and then write the term on the line. Refer to the article for
information. Some have been done for you.

Tiger Woods	Serena Williams	women's golf prize money
Annika Sorenstam	average WNBA salary	men's tennis prize money
average NBA salary	men's golf prize money	women's tennis prize money
Andre Agassi		

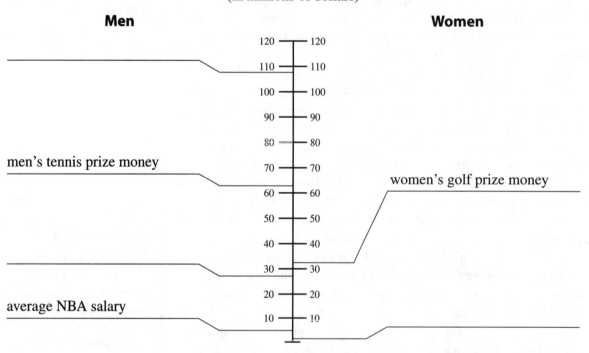

Men's and Women's Professional Sports Earnings
(in millions of dollars)

How does the graph help show the difference between the pay for male and female
athletes? Write two or more sentences to answer this question. When could you use
this type of graph again?

_____

_____

_____

B. Comprehension Skills

Tip! **Think about how to find answers.** Look back at what you read. The information is in the text, but you may have to look in several sentences to find it.

Mark box **a, b,** or **c** with an **X** before the choice that best completes each sentence.

Recalling Facts

1. The pay gap between male and female professional athletes is
   - ☐ **a.** wider than it is in other jobs.
   - ☐ **b.** narrower than it is in other jobs.
   - ☐ **c.** about the same as it is in other jobs.

2. In 2004 the highest-paid female athlete made about
   - ☐ **a.** 6 percent of Tiger Woods's pay.
   - ☐ **b.** 12 percent of Tiger Woods's pay.
   - ☐ **c.** 34 percent of Tiger Woods's pay.

3. The *Forbes* list of the World's 50 Highest-Paid Athletes in 2004 included
   - ☐ **a.** no women.
   - ☐ **b.** 2 women.
   - ☐ **c.** 12 women.

4. Recently the average prize money for women tennis players was about
   - ☐ **a.** 12 percent of men's.
   - ☐ **b.** 34 percent of men's.
   - ☐ **c.** 65 percent of men's.

5. The gap between the average pay for men and women players in basketball is
   - ☐ **a.** wider than the gap in tennis.
   - ☐ **b.** narrower than the gap in tennis.
   - ☐ **c.** about the same as the gap in tennis.

Understanding Ideas

1. From the article, you can conclude that women's sports
   - ☐ **a.** are becoming less popular.
   - ☐ **b.** attract fewer fans than men's sports.
   - ☐ **c.** are less fun than men's sports.

2. The market for women's sports probably
   - ☐ **a.** is shrinking.
   - ☐ **b.** has room to grow.
   - ☐ **c.** has reached its peak.

3. Women in professional sports will make more money as
   - ☐ **a.** women's sports attract more fans.
   - ☐ **b.** more women become professional athletes.
   - ☐ **c.** men's sports begin to lose fans.

4. WNBA players would earn more money if
   - ☐ **a.** NBA players played less often.
   - ☐ **b.** they competed against men.
   - ☐ **c.** the WNBA had more fans.

5. To help improve female athletes' pay, people could
   - ☐ **a.** make new laws.
   - ☐ **b.** put limits on male athletes' pay.
   - ☐ **c.** show more women's sports on television.

C. Reading Strategies

1. Recognizing Words in Context

Find the word *popular* in the article. One definition below is closest to the meaning of that word. One definition has the opposite or nearly the opposite meaning. The remaining definition has a meaning that has nothing to do with the word. Label the definitions **C** for *closest*, **O** for *opposite* or *nearly opposite*, and **U** for *unrelated*.

_____ **a.** strange or unusual to many people

_____ **b.** pleasing or interesting to many people

_____ **c.** boring or unexciting to many people

2. Distinguishing Fact from Opinion

Two of the statements below present *facts,* which can be proved. The other statement is an *opinion,* which expresses someone's thoughts or beliefs. Label the statements **F** for *fact* and **O** for *opinion.*

_____ **a.** Men's sports are more interesting than women's sports.

_____ **b.** Serena Williams makes more money than Annika Sorenstam does.

_____ **c.** In 2003 the NBA paid its players an average of $4.5 million.

3. Making Correct Inferences

Two of the statements below are correct *inferences,* or reasonable guesses, that are based on information in the article. The other statement is an incorrect, or faulty, inference. Label the statements **C** for *correct* inference and **I** for *incorrect* inference.

_____ **a.** If a sport is shown on television, it may affect how much money the athletes make.

_____ **b.** The pay gap between male and female golfers is wider than the pay gap between male and female tennis players.

_____ **c.** Female athletes are not happy with the amount of money they make.

4. Understanding Main Ideas

One of the statements below expresses the main idea of the article. Another statement is too general, or too broad. The other explains only part of the article; it is too narrow. Label the statements **M** for *main idea*, **B** for *too broad*, and **N** for *too narrow.*

_____ **a.** The highest-paid man in sports made $80 million in 2004.

_____ **b.** Female professional athletes make less money than male professional athletes because they attract fewer fans.

_____ **c.** Women often make less money than men do.

5. Responding to the Article

Complete the following sentence in your own words:

What interested me most in "Athletes' Pay: Men Versus Women" was

_____

_____

D. Expanding Vocabulary

Content-Area Words

Complete each sentence with a word from the box. Write the missing word on the line.

gap	earnings	athletes	salary	market

1. A doctor and a lawyer may make the same _____.

2. There is a wide knowledge _____ between a first-grader and a college graduate.

3. All _____ must exercise to stay in good shape.

4. I plan to buy a CD player with my _____ from babysitting.

5. The cell phone _____ has grown quickly in recent years.

Academic English

In the article "Athletes' Pay: Men Versus Women," you learned that *professional* is an adjective that means "having a job that is the source of one's income or money." *Professional* can also be a noun that means "a person who has a certain job or profession," as in the following sentence.

A doctor is a professional who helps people take care of their health.

Complete the sentence below.

1. A *professional* in the field of music must _____

Now use the word *professional* in a sentence of your own.

2. _____

_____

You also learned that *contrast* is a noun that means "a difference between two things." *Contrast* can also be a verb that means "to compare two things in order to see the differences between them," as in the following sentence.

When people contrast the tastes of sugar and salt, they find that sugar is sweeter.

Complete the sentence below.

3. To see which are more comfortable, *contrast* the stiff boots with _____

Now use the word *contrast* in two sentences of your own.

4. _____

5. _____

 Share your new sentences with a partner.

Before You Read

Tip! **Think about what you know.** Read the first and last paragraphs of the article on the opposite page. What do you think the rest of the article may be about? Think about what you already know about paychecks.

Vocabulary

The content-area and academic English words below appear in "DeShawn's Paycheck." Read the definitions and the example sentences.

Content-Area Words

gross (grōs) total
Example: If Ed works 10 hours for $12 per hour, his *gross* pay is $120.

deductions (di duk'shənz) amounts taken away or subtracted from a total
Example: The *deductions* from Ed's paycheck equal $30.

net (net) remaining after all deductions have been made
Example: After $30 is deducted from Ed's $120 gross pay, his *net* pay is $90.

income (in'kum´) money that a person receives as payment for work or services
Example: To earn *income,* I babysit and sell sweaters that I knit myself.

insurance (in shoor'əns) protection against risk or loss; a contract that arranges for a person to pay money in exchange for a company's promise to pay money in the case of problems, such as illness or property damage
Example: My family has *insurance* for our health, our home, and our car.

Academic English

annual (an'ū əl) measured by the year
Example: The *annual* rainfall in the desert is very low.

federal (fed'ər əl) relating to the central government of the United States
Example: The *federal* government pays people to serve in the military.

Read again the example sentences that follow the content-area and academic English word definitions. With a partner, discuss the meanings of the words and sentences. Then make up a sentence of your own for each word.

 Now skim the article and look for other words that are new to you. Write each new word and its definition in the Personal Dictionary.

While You Read

 Think about why you read. Do you think paycheck deductions are a good idea or a bad idea? Write down a question about paycheck deductions that you would like to know the answer to. As you read, try to find the answer.

DeShawn's Paycheck

1 After DeShawn graduates from college, he starts his first full-time job. DeShawn's **annual** salary is $36,036, so his weekly **gross** pay, or his weekly earnings before **deductions,** equals $693 ($36,036 ÷ 52 = $693). When he receives his first paycheck, he is not surprised to see that his **net** pay is much
5 less than $693. He looks at the check record that comes with the paycheck and finds several deductions listed on it. These amounts have been subtracted from DeShawn's gross pay.

The first deduction listed on the check record is for FICA (**Federal** Insurance Contributions Act). This deduction is for Social Security, which is a program
10 that pays money to people who have retired from their jobs. The FICA tax rate on DeShawn's earnings is 7.65 percent. This means that the federal government has deducted $53.01 in FICA tax from DeShawn's paycheck.

Both federal and state **income** taxes also have been deducted from DeShawn's gross pay. People pay federal income tax to the U.S. government to support its
15 work and to fund different national programs. The government has tax tables that show how much money people must pay based on their yearly earnings. DeShawn must pay $3,884 in federal income taxes for the year. That amount, divided by the number of weeks in a year, equals $74.69 per week ($3,884 ÷ 52 = $74.69). State income taxes provide money for state government
20 programs. State taxes also are based on a person's yearly gross income, but the percentage deducted is smaller than it is for the federal income tax. DeShawn's state income tax deduction is $38.19 per week.

The company that DeShawn works for buys basic health **insurance** for workers. This insurance covers major medical costs for workers. People who
25 work for the company can choose to pay extra money to increase the amount of insurance they may receive. Because DeShawn has chosen extra medical and dental insurance, these costs also have been deducted from his pay. He pays $1,404 each year for the extra health insurance, or $27 per week.

DeShawn sees that the last deduction is for his savings plan. This plan lets
30 DeShawn send part of his earnings directly to a savings account at his bank. DeShawn believes that he saves money more easily when it is deducted straight from his paycheck. He has $50 per week deposited, or placed, directly into his savings account. This means that his savings total is $2,600 each year ($50 × 52 = $2,600).

35 The deductions from DeShawn's paycheck total $242.89. DeShawn divides the total deductions by the gross pay of $693. He finds that his weekly deductions equal about 35 percent of his gross pay.

LANGUAGE CONNECTION

In the article, the word *tables* means "charts of organized information or numbers." *Tables* can also mean "pieces of furniture made of a flat surface held up by legs." Which definition are you more familiar with?

CONTENT CONNECTION

Many companies allow workers to use *direct deposit*. This means that the company puts the paycheck money directly into a worker's bank account. Would you rather deposit a paycheck at the bank or use direct deposit? Why?

After You Read

A. Organizing Ideas

What are the purposes of deductions from a paycheck? Complete the web below. In each circle, write down one deduction that may be subtracted from a paycheck. Then write down the purpose of each deduction. Use the article to help you. Some have been done for you.

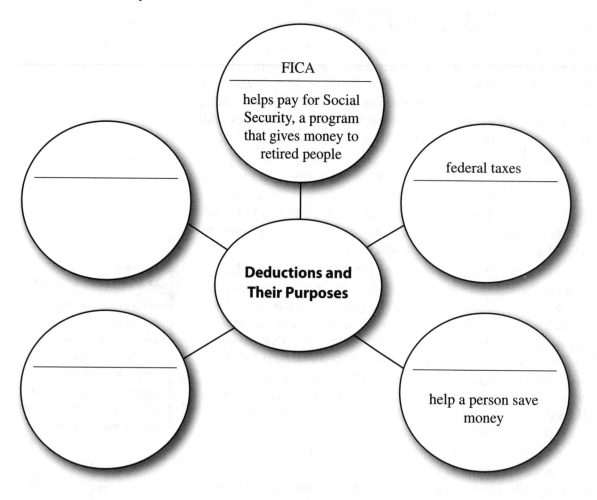

Why do you think it may be important to know what deductions are subtracted from a paycheck? Write two or more sentences to answer this question. How did the web help you answer the question?

_____

_____

_____

_____

B. Comprehension Skills

Tip! **Think about how to find answers.** Read each sentence below. Underline the words that will help you figure out how to complete each item.

Mark box **a, b,** or **c** with an **X** before the choice that best completes each sentence.

Recalling Facts

1. The amounts of money that are subtracted from a paycheck are the
   - ☐ **a.** gross payments.
   - ☐ **b.** FICA totals.
   - ☐ **c.** deductions.

2. The amount of money that a company pays a worker is the
   - ☐ **a.** salary.
   - ☐ **b.** net pay.
   - ☐ **c.** paycheck.

3. A person's earnings before deductions is his or her
   - ☐ **a.** net pay.
   - ☐ **b.** gross pay.
   - ☐ **c.** payroll savings.

4. FICA is the deduction for
   - ☐ **a.** federal income taxes.
   - ☐ **b.** federal health insurance.
   - ☐ **c.** Social Security.

5. The amount of money that is added to DeShawn's savings account each week is
   - ☐ **a.** $50.
   - ☐ **b.** $693.
   - ☐ **c.** $2,600.

Understanding Ideas

1. Deductions from DeShawn's paycheck are
   - ☐ **a.** all for taxes.
   - ☐ **b.** subtracted from his net pay.
   - ☐ **c.** subtracted from his gross pay.

2. The amount of federal income tax that is deducted from DeShawn's paycheck
   - ☐ **a.** pays for all government-funded programs.
   - ☐ **b.** will increase if he makes more money.
   - ☐ **c.** will decrease if he makes more money.

3. Federal and state income taxes
   - ☐ **a.** fund government programs.
   - ☐ **b.** pay benefits to retired people.
   - ☐ **c.** are sent directly to savings accounts.

4. If a worker has a high insurance deduction, it probably means that the company
   - ☐ **a.** pays for all medical costs.
   - ☐ **b.** gives little toward the cost of health insurance.
   - ☐ **c.** gives a large amount toward the cost of heath insurance.

5. If DeShawn wanted fewer deductions from his pay, he could
   - ☐ **a.** stop getting extra medical and dental insurance.
   - ☐ **b.** stop paying state income taxes.
   - ☐ **c.** save more money each week.

C. Reading Strategies

1. Recognizing Words in Context

Find the word *basic* in the article. One definition below is closest to the meaning of that word. One definition has the opposite or nearly the opposite meaning. The remaining definition has a meaning that has nothing to do with the word. Label the definitions **C** for *closest*, **O** for *opposite* or *nearly opposite*, and **U** for *unrelated*.

_____ **a.** simple

_____ **b.** including many extra things

_____ **c.** causing too many problems

2. Distinguishing Fact from Opinion

Two of the statements below present *facts*, which can be proved. The other statement is an *opinion*, which expresses someone's thoughts or beliefs. Label the statements **F** for *fact* and **O** for *opinion*.

_____ **a.** Some paycheck deductions pay for programs that help other people.

_____ **b.** People should purchase more insurance than their company provides.

_____ **c.** Deductions may help people save their money.

3. Making Correct Inferences

Two of the statements below are correct *inferences*, or reasonable guesses, that are based on information in the article. The other statement is an incorrect, or faulty, inference. Label the statements **C** for *correct* inference and **I** for *incorrect* inference.

_____ **a.** People with high incomes provide more money for government programs than people with low incomes do.

_____ **b.** People must have savings account deductions in order to save money.

_____ **c.** Medical expenses would be very high for most people if they did not have health insurance.

4. Understanding Main Ideas

One of the statements below expresses the main idea of the article. Another statement is too general, or too broad. The other explains only part of the article; it is too narrow. Label the statements **M** for *main idea*, **B** for *too broad*, and **N** for *too narrow*.

_____ **a.** Deductions from paychecks go toward things such as taxes, insurance, and savings.

_____ **b.** Because of deductions, a worker receives only part of his or her salary.

_____ **c.** Federal and state governments take money from paychecks to pay for programs.

5. Responding to the Article

Complete the following sentence in your own words:

One thing in "DeShawn's Paycheck" that I cannot understand is

_____

_____

D. Expanding Vocabulary

Content-Area Words

Read each item carefully. Write on the line the word or phrase that best completes each sentence.

1. Income is money that people receive when they _____.
   do work   become sick   leave a job

2. People purchase insurance to help pay for _____.
   taxes   clothes   medical expenses

3. The amount of money that a person earns _____ is the gross pay.
   in a month   before deductions   after deductions

4. The amounts of money that _____ a paycheck are the deductions.
   are subtracted from   are added to   are included in

5. A person's net pay is the amount of money in a _____.
   paycheck   deduction   savings account

Academic English

In the article "DeShawn's Paycheck," you learned that *annual* means "measured by the year." *Annual* can also mean "taking place once each year," as in the following sentence.

   I have an annual appointment with my doctor to check my health.

Complete the sentence below.

1. My favorite *annual* holiday is _____

Now use the word *annual* in a sentence of your own.

2. _____

   _____

You also learned that *federal* means "relating to the central government of the United States." *Federal* can refer to government taxes. *Federal* can also refer to people and things that are part of the U.S. government, as in the following sentence.

   The United States Postal Service is the federal mail service.

Complete the sentence below.

3. The head of the *federal* government in the United States is the _____

Now use the word *federal* in two sentences of your own.

4. _____

5. _____

 Talk It Over Share your new sentences with a partner.

The Money Behind the Movies

Before You Read

Tip! **Think about what you know.** Read the title and the first paragraph of the article on the opposite page. What do you think the article will be about? What do you already know about what it costs to make a movie?

Vocabulary

The content-area and academic English words below appear in "The Money Behind the Movies." Read the definitions and the example sentences.

Content-Area Words

budget (buj′it) a plan to use a certain amount of money for a set purpose
Example: Rana always makes a *budget* before she plans a party.

expenses (iks pens′əz) items or services that people must spend money on
Example: My school *expenses* include paper, pencils, and books.

production (prə duk′shən) the process of making something
Example: The *production* of our school play took many months.

profit (prof′it) the money that remains after a business has paid all of its costs
Example: The company reduced its costs in order to earn a higher *profit*.

ratio (rā′shē ō′) a comparison in size or amount between two things
Example: The *ratio* of wins to losses for our team was 2 to 1 this year.

Academic English

vary (vār′ē) to be different
Example: The weather will *vary* from cold to warm during the spring season.

category (kat′ə gôr′ē) a group of things within a larger system
Example: Tigers are one *category* of cats.

Answer the questions below. Circle the part of each question that is the answer. The first one has been done for you.

1. To find the *ratio* of cows to horses, would someone (compare the numbers of cows and horses) or count the number of horses?
2. Are oaks a *category* of trees or of animals?
3. Would *expenses* for family pets be food and medicine or sleep and play?
4. Does a *budget* help people decide what to eat or how to spend money?
5. If a person's emotions *vary*, do they change often or stay the same?
6. Does the *production* of a movie involve ticket sales or actors' salaries?
7. To make a *profit*, should a business spend more money than it makes or make more money than it spends?

 Now skim the article and look for other words that are new to you. Write each new word and its definition in the Personal Dictionary.

While You Read

 Think about why you read. Can you think of a movie that probably cost many millions of dollars to make? Movie studios want to make money, but first they need to spend money. As you read, look for the different expenses that movie studios have as they make movies.

$The Money Behind the Movies

1 A Hollywood movie studio may spend $250 million or more to make a film, or movie. However, the studio may spend as little as $200,000. The first is a high-**budget** film, and the second is a low-budget film. A studio creates a budget for every film so that it can figure out how much the movie will cost to make.

5 Film budgets include two types of costs. Costs such as the salaries for writers, directors, producers, and top actors appear in the higher part of the budget. These are called *above-the-line costs*. The crew, supplies, advertising, and other costs related to the film appear in the lower part of the budget. These are called *below-the-line costs*.

10 Different kinds of films need different kinds of budgets, because **expenses vary** for each type of film. The budget for a cartoon movie includes salaries for actors to do the voices of characters. It also includes salaries for artists to draw the characters. An action film with special effects usually costs more than a romantic comedy. Studios have to figure out how much money they will spend
15 in each **category** of the budget. For example, studios often spend $50 million or more to advertise a movie. The advertising budget for *The Lord of the Rings: The Return of the King* was $75 million in the United States alone.

Budgets allow studios to understand exactly what they are spending on a film per minute. If the film has a **production** budget of $15 million and is 100 minutes
20 long, each minute of the film costs $150,000 to make ($15,000,000 ÷ 100 = $150,000). Studios spend a lot of money, but they also hope to earn a **profit.**

To figure out how successful a movie is, studios look at the profit **ratio** of the film. This ratio compares the gross profit of the movie to its budget. The gross profit of the movie is the amount it earns in ticket sales. The goals of the studio
25 are to keep the cost of the film down and to keep the ticket sales up. To calculate profit ratio, divide the gross profit of the film by the cost of its production. For example, a film that has a gross profit of $420 million and a production budget of $50 million has a profit ratio of 8.4 (420 ÷ 50 = 8.4). The movie *Titanic* had a gross profit of $600 million. It cost $200 million to make. That is a profit ratio
30 of 3 (600 ÷ 200 = 3). Since 1990, only 15 movies with total ticket sales of at least $20 million have had profit ratios higher than 10.

LANGUAGE CONNECTION

In *film budgets,* the noun *film* acts as an adjective. *Film* describes a specific kind of budget. Try to find other nouns that act as adjectives in the article. Hint: Look at line 22.

CONTENT CONNECTION

The Indian film industry is the largest in the world. In 2002 India released 1,200 movies. People throughout the world are beginning to enjoy Indian films. Have you seen any movies that were made in another country?

After You Read

A. Organizing Ideas

How do people calculate the important numbers in the movie business? Complete the chart below. In the left column, list numbers that movie studios must calculate. In the right column, write sentences to explain how each number is calculated. Use the article to find information. Some have been done for you.

The Numbers of the Movie Business

Number	How It Is Calculated
above-the-line costs	Add together the salaries for writers, directors, producers, and top actors.
production budget	
cost per minute	
	Multiply the number of tickets sold by the ticket prices.
profit ratio	

What did you learn about the numbers in the movie business? Write two or more sentences to answer this question. Did the chart help you answer the question? Why or why not?

_____

_____

_____

_____

_____

B. Comprehension Skills

Tip! **Think about how to find answers.** Look back at what you read. The words in an answer are usually contained in a single sentence.

Mark box **a, b,** or **c** with an **X** before the choice that best completes each sentence.

Recalling Facts

1. The above-the-line costs for a film include
   - ☐ **a.** advertising costs.
   - ☐ **b.** the costs of labor and supplies.
   - ☐ **c.** salaries for writers, directors, producers, and top actors.

2. Action films usually have
   - ☐ **a.** low profit ratios.
   - ☐ **b.** lower costs than romantic comedies.
   - ☐ **c.** special effects costs.

3. A film that costs less than $1 million to make is a
   - ☐ **a.** boring film.
   - ☐ **b.** low-budget film.
   - ☐ **c.** high-budget film.

4. To calculate the profit ratio of a movie, divide the movie's
   - ☐ **a.** gross profit by its production cost.
   - ☐ **b.** budget by its gross profit.
   - ☐ **c.** above-the-line costs by its below-the-line costs.

5. To find the profit ratio of a movie that earned $600 million and cost $200 million,
   - ☐ **a.** divide 600 by 200.
   - ☐ **b.** divide 200 by 600.
   - ☐ **c.** multiply 600 by 200.

Understanding Ideas

1. To find the cost per minute of a film, divide
   - ☐ **a.** the cost by the gross profit.
   - ☐ **b.** the cost by the number of minutes.
   - ☐ **c.** the number of minutes by the cost.

2. A movie studio tries to keep its
   - ☐ **a.** profit ratio low.
   - ☐ **b.** costs low and ticket sales high.
   - ☐ **c.** budget equal to the gross profit.

3. From the article, you can conclude that
   - ☐ **a.** movie studios should keep advertising costs low.
   - ☐ **b.** advertising always increases the profit ratio of a film.
   - ☐ **c.** advertising is an important part of the budget for a film.

4. It is not true that
   - ☐ **a.** high-budget films always have a high gross profit.
   - ☐ **b.** gross profit depends on the number of tickets that are sold.
   - ☐ **c.** a film's gross profit continues to go up as long as it runs in theaters.

5. If a film has a profit ratio of 10, the movie studio people are likely to be
   - ☐ **a.** very pleased.
   - ☐ **b.** disappointed.
   - ☐ **c.** somewhat pleased.

C. Reading Strategies

1. Recognizing Words in Context

Find the word *advertise* in the article. One definition below is closest to the meaning of that word. One definition has the opposite or nearly the opposite meaning. The remaining definition has a meaning that has nothing to do with the word. Label the definitions **C** for *closest*, **O** for *opposite* or *nearly opposite*, and **U** for *unrelated*.

_____ **a.** to give product information to the public

_____ **b.** to learn information about the public

_____ **c.** to keep product information secret from the public

2. Distinguishing Fact from Opinion

Two of the statements below present *facts*, which can be proved. The other statement is an *opinion*, which expresses someone's thoughts or beliefs. Label the statements **F** for *fact* and **O** for *opinion*.

_____ **a.** High-budget movies are better than low-budget movies.

_____ **b.** A high profit ratio means that the production budget was much less than the gross profit of a movie.

_____ **c.** Different types of films have different types of costs.

3. Making Correct Inferences

Two of the statements below are correct *inferences,* or reasonable guesses, that are based on information in the article. The other statement is an incorrect, or faulty, inference. Label the statements **C** for *correct* inference and **I** for *incorrect* inference.

_____ **a.** A film with a low production budget will definitely have a high profit ratio.

_____ **b.** A short movie with a high production budget has a high cost per minute.

_____ **c.** Salaries may be a large part of the budget if a film has famous actors.

4. Understanding Main Ideas

One of the statements below expresses the main idea of the article. Another statement is too general, or too broad. The other explains only part of the article; it is too narrow. Label the statements **M** for *main idea*, **B** for *too broad*, and **N** for *too narrow*.

_____ **a.** The production budget of a film includes everything it costs to make the film.

_____ **b.** Film studios use budgets to help them organize costs as they try to make a profit.

_____ **c.** Film studios hope to earn a profit when they make a film.

5. Responding to the Article

Complete the following sentence in your own words:

Reading "The Money Behind the Movies" made me want to learn more about

_____

_____

because _____

_____

D. Expanding Vocabulary

Content-Area Words

Complete each analogy with a word from the box. Write in the missing word.

budget	expenses	production	profit	ratio

1. profits : earn :: _____ : pay

2. sum : addition :: _____ : comparison

3. construction : house :: _____ : movie

4. schedule : time :: _____ : money

5. grow : shrink :: _____ : loss

Academic English

In the article "The Money Behind the Movies," you learned that *vary* means "to be different." *Vary* can also mean "to choose different kinds of something," as in the following sentence.

People usually vary the foods they eat for different meals.

Complete the sentence below.

1. People *vary* the clothing they wear according to _____

Now use the word *vary* in a sentence of your own.

2. _____

_____

You also learned that *category* means "a group of things within a larger system." *Category* can refer to a group of costs within a budget. *Category* can also refer to other groups within larger systems, as in the following sentence.

Roses are a category of flowers.

Complete the sentence below.

3. My favorite *category* of music is _____

Now use the word *category* in two sentences of your own.

4. _____

5. _____

 Share your new sentences with a partner.

Before You Read

 Think about what you know. Read the title and the first three sentences of the second paragraph of the article on the opposite page. Think about what you already know about voting and about how U.S. citizens choose their president.

Vocabulary

The content-area and academic English words below appear in "The Electoral College." Read the definitions and the example sentences.

Content-Area Words

election (i lek´shən) an event at which people vote to choose a person for a position
 Example: The students held an *election* to choose class officers.

senators (sen´ə tərz) elected members of the U.S. Senate
 Example: Each state elects two *senators* to the U.S. Congress.

representatives (rep´ri zen´tə tivz) elected members of the U.S. House of Representatives
 Example: Most people vote for *representatives* who share their views.

population (pop´yə lā´shən) the number of people who live in a certain place
 Example: The state of California has a large *population*.

candidate (kan´də dit) a person who seeks to be elected to a certain office or position
 Example: A *candidate* for class president should be a good leader.

Academic English

allocated (al´ə kāt´əd) set aside or gave for a certain purpose
 Example: Teresa *allocated* time each night to do her homework.

minimum (min´ə məm) the smallest necessary amount of something
 Example: I need a *minimum* of 20 minutes to get ready for school.

Rate each vocabulary word according to the following scale. Write a number next to each content-area and academic English word.

4   I have never seen the word before.

3   I have seen the word but do not know what it means.

2   I know what the word means when I read it.

1   I use the word myself in speaking or writing.

 Now skim the article and look for other words that are new to you. Write each new word and its definition in the Personal Dictionary.

While You Read

Tip! **Think about why you read.** What do you want to learn about the electoral college? Before you read, turn to the next page. Fill in the first two columns of the chart with facts that you know and questions that you have about the electoral college. As you read, look for answers to your questions.

The Electoral College

1 Imagine this common situation. A teacher gives her students two choices for a field trip. The choices are a trip to the science museum or a visit to a nearby university. The teacher allows the class to decide, so the students vote. The class has 31 students. Eighteen students, or more than half, vote for the trip to the

5 science museum. Because it receives more votes than the other choice does, this choice is the winner.

In the U.S. presidential **election** in 2000, Al Gore received 50,999,897 votes, and George W. Bush received 50,456,002 votes. Gore received 543,895 more votes than Bush did. However, George W. Bush became president. Why? In the United

10 States, the president is not elected by the total number of votes. The electoral college, a group of people that represent the citizens of their states, selects the president. The word *college* comes from a Latin word that means "society."

The people who wrote the U.S. Constitution created the electoral college in 1787. To each state, they **allocated** a certain number of electoral votes based on

15 two factors. They gave each state one vote for each senator. This means that each state has two votes, because each state has two U.S. **senators.** The other electoral votes come from the number of U.S. **representatives** in each state. The **population** of the state determines this number. States with high populations have more electoral votes than states with low populations do.

20 California, for example, has 55 electoral votes. This is about 20 percent of the total electoral votes that a presidential **candidate** needs in order to win an election. If a candidate loses in California, he or she will probably need to win in several other states just to equal the number of electoral votes in California.

In electoral college voting, a candidate wins all of the electoral votes in a state

25 if that candidate wins the popular vote, or gets the most total votes, in that state. The total number of electoral votes from all of the states is 538. A candidate must receive a **minimum** of 270, or one more than half of all the electoral votes, to win the election.

Except for four times in U.S. history, the winners of the electoral college vote

30 have also won the popular vote. In 2000 the election was very close. Before the votes in Florida were decided, Bush had a total of 246 electoral college votes and Gore had 266. Both candidates needed the electoral college votes in Florida to win. After people counted the popular vote in Florida, the Florida electoral votes went to George W. Bush. His total went up to 271 electoral votes, and he

35 became the 43rd U.S. president.

LANGUAGE CONNECTION

The noun *election* is related to the verb *elect,* which means "to choose by voting." Try to find another word in the article that is related to the verb *elect.* What part of speech is it?

CONTENT CONNECTION

Imagine that three candidates run for president, and none of them receive 270 electoral votes. In this case, the House of Representatives elects the president. Do you think this is fair? Why or why not?

After You Read

A. Organizing Ideas

What do you know or want to know about the U.S. electoral college? Complete the chart below. List four facts that you already know about the electoral college and four things that you want to learn about. After you read the article, list four facts that you learned from the article.

The U.S. Electoral College

What I Know	What I Want to Know	What I Have Learned

Did this chart help you learn more about something that you already knew? Write two or more sentences about something new that you have learned. How could you use this type of chart again? Explain your answer.

_____

_____

_____

B. Comprehension Skills

Tip! **Think about how to find answers.** Look back at different parts of the text. What facts help you figure out how to complete the sentences?

Mark box **a, b,** or **c** with an **X** before the choice that best completes each sentence.

Recalling Facts

1. People created the electoral college in
   - ☐ **a.** 1776.
   - ☐ **b.** 1787.
   - ☐ **c.** 2000.

2. In the 2000 election, Gore received
   - ☐ **a.** 270 more votes than Bush did.
   - ☐ **b.** 538 more votes than Bush did.
   - ☐ **c.** almost 544,000 more votes than Bush did.

3. To win the 2000 election, Bush received
   - ☐ **a.** 271 electoral college votes.
   - ☐ **b.** 270 electoral college votes.
   - ☐ **c.** 266 electoral college votes.

4. The number of electoral votes that a state has is equal to the state's
   - ☐ **a.** number of U.S. senators.
   - ☐ **b.** number of U.S. representatives.
   - ☐ **c.** number of U.S. senators and U.S. representatives.

5. Both Gore and Bush needed Florida's electoral votes because neither candidate
   - ☐ **a.** was ahead in electoral votes.
   - ☐ **b.** had 270 electoral votes.
   - ☐ **c.** had more of the popular vote.

Understanding Ideas

1. From the article, you can conclude that people created the electoral college to
   - ☐ **a.** take away people's voting rights.
   - ☐ **b.** give states with small populations a stronger role in elections.
   - ☐ **c.** make states with large populations more important in elections.

2. A candidate who wins the popular vote
   - ☐ **a.** cannot win the election.
   - ☐ **b.** always wins the election.
   - ☐ **c.** may not win the election.

3. A candidate for president wins the electoral votes of a state
   - ☐ **a.** no matter who wins the popular vote in the state.
   - ☐ **b.** if the candidate wins the popular vote in the state.
   - ☐ **c.** if the candidate needs the electoral votes to win the election.

4. It is not true that
   - ☐ **a.** electoral votes are important only in a close election.
   - ☐ **b.** a state with few electoral votes may make a difference in an election.
   - ☐ **c.** a state has the same number of electoral votes no matter how many people vote.

5. A state's number of electoral college votes may change if
   - ☐ **a.** its population grows.
   - ☐ **b.** it votes for one candidate.
   - ☐ **c.** it encourages more people to vote.

C. Reading Strategies

1. Recognizing Words in Context

Find the word *common* in the article. One definition below is closest to the meaning of that word. One definition has the opposite or nearly the opposite meaning. The remaining definition has a meaning that has nothing to do with the word. Label the definitions **C** for *closest*, **O** for *opposite* or *nearly opposite*, and **U** for *unrelated*.

_____ **a.** strange

_____ **b.** recent

_____ **c.** usual

2. Distinguishing Fact from Opinion

Two of the statements below present *facts*, which can be proved. The other statement is an *opinion*, which expresses someone's thoughts or beliefs. Label the statements **F** for *fact* and **O** for *opinion*.

_____ **a.** A candidate who wins the popular vote may lose the presidential election.

_____ **b.** The number of U.S. representatives in a state depends on the population of the state.

_____ **c.** The U.S. president should be elected by popular vote.

3. Making Correct Inferences

Two of the statements below are correct *inferences*, or reasonable guesses, that are based on information in the article. The other statement is an incorrect, or faulty, inference. Label the statements **C** for *correct* inference and **I** for *incorrect* inference.

_____ **a.** Each state has more than two electoral votes.

_____ **b.** The popular vote does not matter in the presidential election.

_____ **c.** A small state with only a few electoral votes may be important in an election.

4. Understanding Main Ideas

One of the statements below expresses the main idea of the article. Another statement is too general, or too broad. The other explains only part of the article; it is too narrow. Label the statements **M** for *main idea*, **B** for *too broad*, and **N** for *too narrow*.

_____ **a.** A presidential candidate needs at least 270 electoral votes to win the election.

_____ **b.** U.S. citizens choose their president by voting in elections.

_____ **c.** The electoral college represents the states and elects the U.S. president.

5. Responding to the Article

Complete the following sentence in your own words:

Before reading "The Electoral College," I already knew

_____

_____

D. Expanding Vocabulary

Content-Area Words

Cross out one word or phrase in each row that is not related to the word in dark type.

1. election	learn	choose	votes	president
2. senators	state	judge	two	elected
3. representatives	elected	electoral votes	population	two
4. population	state	license	citizens	number
5. candidate	election	office	votes	ratio

Academic English

In the article "The Electoral College," you learned that *allocated* means "set aside or gave for a certain purpose." In the article, *allocated* refers to the electoral votes given to each state for the presidential election. *Allocated* can also refer to other things set aside or given for a purpose, as in the following sentence.

The park allocated half of the money from the festival to the new playground fund.

Complete the sentence below.

1. The school *allocated* a locker _____

Now use the word *allocated* in a sentence of your own.

2. _____

_____

You also learned that *minimum* means "the smallest necessary amount of something." *Minimum* can also mean "the lowest point reached," as in the following sentence.

The level of water in a lake is at its minimum during dry months.

Complete the sentence below.

3. The company's pen sales were at a *minimum* after people said that _____

Now use the word *minimum* in two sentences of your own.

4. _____

5. _____

 Share your new sentences with a partner.

Before You Read

 Think about what you know. Read the first paragraph of the article on the opposite page. Why do you think people from many other countries come to live in the United States?

Vocabulary

The content-area and academic English words below appear in "The Success of Vietnamese Americans." Read the definitions and the example sentences.

Content-Area Words

generation (jen´ə rā′shən) a group of people that makes up one step in a family line
Example: My sister and I belong to the younger *generation* of our family.

prejudice (prej´ə dis) dislike of a group such as a race or religion
Example: People may feel *prejudice* toward a certain religion if they do not understand it.

industry (in′dəs trē) a branch of business, trade, or production
Example: Fashion designers work in the clothing *industry*.

retail (rē′tāl) the sale of items in small amounts directly to the customer
Example: Grocery stores and music stores are *retail* businesses.

ethnic (eth′nik) relating to a group of people who share a culture, race, or history
Example: The two Japanese students have similar *ethnic* backgrounds.

Academic English

statistics (stə tis′tiks) the collection and study of numbers that relate to certain subjects
Example: The scientist uses *statistics* to predict when volcanoes may erupt.

immigrant (im′ə grənt) a person who enters a new country and plans to stay there permanently
Example: Jean-Louis is an *immigrant* to the United States from Haiti.

Do any of the words above seem related? Sort the seven vocabulary words into two or more categories. Write the words down on note cards or in a chart. Words may fit into more than one group. You may wish to work with a partner for this activity. Label one category *Groups of People*.

Dictionary Now skim the article and look for other words that are new to you. Write each new word and its definition in the Personal Dictionary.

While You Read

Tip! **Think about why you read.** What things may help an immigrant to succeed? As you read, look for reasons why Vietnamese Americans are considered to be successful immigrants.

The Success of Vietnamese Americans

1   The families of many Vietnamese Americans began to arrive in the United States in the 1960s and continued to arrive through the 1980s. Many made the move because of war in their home country. All of them were looking for a better life. Today more than one million Vietnamese Americans live in the
5   United States. People can study this success story through **statistics.**

Statistics is a branch of mathematics. It uses numbers to look at "little pictures" of the world. These "little pictures" help people understand the world's "big pictures." With statistics, people can learn a great deal about the experience of Vietnamese Americans in this country.

10   A study done in California in the year 2000 reported that most Vietnamese Americans live in California. Texas has the second-largest number of Vietnamese Americans, with large communities in Houston, Dallas, and Austin. The state of Washington has the third-largest number of Vietnamese Americans.

The statistics also showed that 11 percent of all Vietnamese Americans are
15   self-employed, which means that they own their own businesses. The study suggested that as many as 99 percent of these business owners are first-**generation** Americans. *First-generation* refers to people born in Vietnam who moved to the United States. This group of people faced two big problems when they came to America. First, they could not speak English. Second, like many
20   other **immigrant** groups, they faced **prejudice.** They were not able to get many jobs—and most of the jobs they could get paid low wages. They had a better chance for success if they started their own businesses.

The same study reported that about 64 percent of Vietnamese American businesses are part of the service **industry.** These businesses include beauty
25   shops and barbershops, laundry services, and health care clinics. Another 24 percent of the businesses are **retail** businesses, such as restaurants, grocery stores, and small shops. Half of the business owners said that more than 75 percent of their customers are "**ethnic** customers." In this case, *ethnic* is likely to mean "mostly Vietnamese American."

30   These numbers show that most of the opportunities for first-generation Vietnamese immigrants are within their own ethnic communities. The statistics are different for second- and third-generation Vietnamese Americans. Why? Perhaps because hard work and education are the keys to success in the United States. Vietnamese American adults have worked hard to make sure that their
35   children could get a better education in the United States than they did. They have encouraged their children to study hard so that they could go to college. Statistics suggest that Vietnamese Americans are an American success story.

LANGUAGE CONNECTION

The phrase *a great deal* means "a large, but not definite, amount." What are some things that a person may have a great deal of?

CONTENT CONNECTION

The Immigration Act of 1965 allowed more immigrants to enter the United States from Third World countries. Do you know of any other laws that affect immigrants?

After You Read

A. Organizing Ideas

What conclusions can people make from statistics about Vietnamese Americans? Complete the chart below. In the left column, list statistics from the article about Vietnamese Americans. In the right column, write down conclusions about Vietnamese Americans that you can make from each statistic. Some have been done for you.

Statistics About Vietnamese Americans	Conclusions
	Two of these states border the ocean, which makes it easier for immigrants to travel to them. They are all located on the western side of the United States, which is closer to Asia.
Numbers show that 11% of Vietnamese Americans own their own businesses.	Vietnamese immigrants may have found it difficult to get good jobs due to language problems and prejudice, so they started their own businesses.
	These industries allowed Vietnamese Americans to make money and to serve other immigrants without language problems or prejudice.
More than 75% of the customers at half of Vietnamese American businesses may be Vietnamese American.	

What have you learned about Vietnamese Americans? Why do you think the article refers to them as "an American success story"? Write two or more sentences to answer these questions. Did the chart help you answer the questions? Why or why not?

_____

_____

_____

B. Comprehension Skills

Tip! **Think about how to find answers.** Think about what each sentence means. Try to say it to yourself in your own words before you complete it.

Mark box **a, b,** or **c** with an **X** before the choice that best completes each sentence.

Recalling Facts

1. Most Vietnamese Americans live in
   - ☐ **a.** Texas.
   - ☐ **b.** California.
   - ☐ **c.** Washington.

2. The phrase that best describes *statistics* is
   - ☐ **a.** "a way to count people."
   - ☐ **b.** "numbers that help people understand the world."
   - ☐ **c.** "a branch of mathematics that shows how people earn money."

3. A first-generation Vietnamese American
   - ☐ **a.** was born in Vietnam.
   - ☐ **b.** is the child of an immigrant.
   - ☐ **c.** was born in the United States.

4. Statistics show that
   - ☐ **a.** most Vietnamese Americans own restaurants.
   - ☐ **b.** 11 percent of Vietnamese Americans are self-employed.
   - ☐ **c.** 99 percent of Vietnamese Americans own their own businesses.

5. In a Vietnamese American neighborhood, *ethnic* is likely to describe any person
   - ☐ **a.** who is not Asian American.
   - ☐ **b.** who is not Vietnamese.
   - ☐ **c.** who is Vietnamese American.

Understanding Ideas

1. Many first-generation Vietnamese Americans
   - ☐ **a.** liked to cook and to own shops.
   - ☐ **b.** made their children work with them.
   - ☐ **c.** did not speak English well enough to get a good job.

2. People who face prejudice often
   - ☐ **a.** do not speak English.
   - ☐ **b.** are treated well.
   - ☐ **c.** are treated unfairly.

3. The "American Dream" is probably the idea that
   - ☐ **a.** life in America is easy.
   - ☐ **b.** anything is possible in America if a person works hard.
   - ☐ **c.** a person needs a college education in order to be successful.

4. The article provides examples of
   - ☐ **a.** the best businesses to start today.
   - ☐ **b.** the most common businesses started by Vietnamese Americans.
   - ☐ **c.** industries in which Vietnamese Americans must speak English.

5. Most Vietnamese American businesses
   - ☐ **a.** serve only their ethnic customers.
   - ☐ **b.** sell things that people in the community want.
   - ☐ **c.** provide services that people in the community need.

C. Reading Strategies

1. Recognizing Words in Context

Find the word *suggested* in the article. One definition below is closest to the meaning of that word. One definition has the opposite or nearly the opposite meaning. The remaining definition has a meaning that has nothing to do with the word. Label the definitions **C** for *closest*, **O** for *opposite* or *nearly opposite*, and **U** for *unrelated*.

_____ **a.** organized information to make it easier to understand

_____ **b.** provided information that leads to a conclusion

_____ **c.** hid information in order to cause confusion

2. Distinguishing Fact from Opinion

Two of the statements below present *facts,* which can be proved. The other statement is an *opinion,* which expresses someone's thoughts or beliefs. Label the statements **F** for *fact* and **O** for *opinion.*

_____ **a.** Most Vietnamese American business owners are first-generation Americans.

_____ **b.** Second- and third-generation Vietnamese Americans should seek jobs where they may speak English.

_____ **c.** Vietnamese American businesses are mostly part of the service industry.

3. Making Correct Inferences

Two of the statements below are correct *inferences,* or reasonable guesses, that are based on information in the article. The other statement is an incorrect, or faulty, inference. Label the statements **C** for *correct* inference and **I** for *incorrect* inference.

_____ **a.** Vietnamese immigrants believed that America offered more opportunities.

_____ **b.** A college education may help second- and third-generation Vietnamese Americans get better jobs.

_____ **c.** Most Vietnamese American business owners once ran businesses in Vietnam.

4. Understanding Main Ideas

One of the statements below expresses the main idea of the article. Another statement is too general, or too broad. The other explains only part of the article; it is too narrow. Label the statements **M** for *main idea,* **B** for *too broad,* and **N** for *too narrow.*

_____ **a.** Many first-generation Vietnamese Americans started their own businesses.

_____ **b.** Statistics show that Vietnamese Americans have become successful in the United States through hard work and education.

_____ **c.** Many Vietnamese Americans have succeeded in the United States.

5. Responding to the Article

Complete the following sentence in your own words:

From reading "The Success of Vietnamese Americans," I have learned

_____

_____

D. Expanding Vocabulary

Content-Area Words

Complete each sentence with a word from the box. Write the missing word on the line.

generation	prejudice	industry	retail	ethnic

1. People who show _____ may treat others badly.

2. Jane works in the automobile _____ because she likes cars.

3. People in the same _____ group often speak the same language.

4. Restaurants and stores are _____ businesses.

5. My parents, aunts, and uncles are all part of the same _____.

Academic English

In the article "The Success of Vietnamese Americans," you learned that *statistics* means "the collection and study of numbers that relate to certain subjects." *Statistics* can also mean "numbers that relate to a specific subject," as in the following sentence.

   Baseball statistics give information about a player's performance.

Complete the sentence below.

1. Each state has *statistics* about its citizens, such as _____

Now use the word *statistics* in a sentence of your own.

2. _____

_____

You also learned that *immigrant* is a noun that means "a person who enters a new country and plans to stay there permanently." *Immigrant* can also be an adjective that means "relating to people who are immigrants," as in the following sentence.

   New York City has a large immigrant population.

Complete the sentence below.

3. People in *immigrant* communities are likely to enjoy similar _____

Now use the word *immigrant* in two sentences of your own.

4. _____

5. _____

 Share your new sentences with a partner.

Writing a News Article

Read the news article. Then complete the sentences. Use words from the Word Bank.

Daily News • Math

Future Jobs Will Provide Higher (1)_____

Will doctors in the future make more money than doctors do today? Mathematicians have collected

(2)_____ that show that the

(3)_____ salary for a job in 2020 will be 15% higher than the salary for the same job today. They believe that salaries will go up

in every job (4)_____, but some will go up more than others. In any case, the next

(5)_____ of workers will have plenty of educational and job opportunities.

Word Bank

statistics   annual

earnings   category

generation

Reading a Brochure

Read the brochure. Circle the word that completes each sentence.

Learn How to Make the Most of Your Money!

When you have a job, will you save money? You will probably receive a paycheck either every week or twice per month. If you arrange for a small amount of each check to be (**allocated, candidate**) to your savings account, it will be worth it. Every month you will have (**deductions, expenses**) such as food, rent,

and car (**production, insurance**). But if you save some of your (**income, budget**), you will have money left for the things you want. These things (**vary, retail**) from person to person. Enjoy the things you buy with the money you save!

Saving money is the smart thing to do!

Making Connections

Work with a partner. Talk about what the words mean and how they are connected. Write down pairs of words or single words in each section of the pie. Add notes to explain how the words are related to each other.

| professional | salary | gap | minimum | federal |
| contrast | ratio | immigrant | population | ethnic |

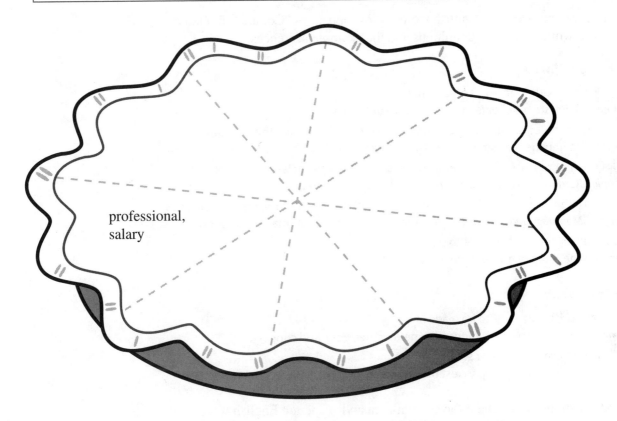

professional,
salary

Use all of the words above in complete sentences of your own. Each sentence may include one or more of the words. To help you start writing, look at the ideas you wrote about. After you write your sentences, read them over. If you find a mistake, correct it.

_____

_____

_____

_____

_____

_____

Before You Read

Tip! **Think about what you know.** Read the title and the first sentence of the article on the opposite page. What do you think the article may be about? Have you ever seen beadwork that has been made by Native Americans or other craftspeople?

Vocabulary

The content-area and academic English words below appear in "Counting in Native American Beadwork." Read the definitions and the example sentences.

Content-Area Words

detail (dē´tāl) small parts or features of an item
Example: Shiny stones of different colors add *detail* to jewelry.

combination (kom´bə nā´shen) a mixture; something formed by putting things together
Example: Lemonade is a *combination* of lemon juice, water, and sugar.

geometric (jē´ə met´rik) made of lines, angles, and shapes such as circles and triangles
Example: Ramiro's shirt has a *geometric* triangle pattern printed on it.

manufactured (man´yə fak´chərd) made in large amounts, usually with the help of machines
Example: *Manufactured* clothes take less time to make than handmade clothes do.

width (width) measurement from side to side
Example: The *width* of my bedroom is 10 feet.

Academic English

comprise (kəm prīz´) to include; to be made of
Example: The necklace will *comprise* the metals silver, gold, and copper.

require (ri kwīr´) to have a need for something
Example: People *require* sleep to rest their bodies.

Answer the questions below about the content-area and academic English words. Write your answers in the spaces provided. The first one has been done for you.

1. What word goes with *a CD that includes different songs?* _____comprise_____
2. What word goes with *a pattern made of sharp angles?* _____
3. What word goes with *something made in a factory?* _____
4. What word goes with *a mixture of different colors?* _____
5. What word goes with *the need for food and water?* _____
6. What word goes with *small parts of a story?* _____
7. What word goes with *how wide something is?* _____

 Dictionary Now skim the article and look for other words that are new to you. Write each new word and its definition in the Personal Dictionary.

While You Read

Tip! **Think about why you read.** Do you own any clothing or jewelry that has beadwork? How do you think beadwork and math are related? As you read, try to answer this question.

Counting in Native American Beadwork

1 People have made things with beads for thousands of years. Some beads are more than 10,000 years old. People have often used beads to embellish craftwork and clothing. *Embellish* means "to add **detail** in order to decorate or improve something." Native Americans have worked with beads throughout
5 their history. They have made beads from many different natural materials, such as shells, stones, ivory, clay, seeds, wood, and bone.

Beadwork is a **combination** of types and patterns of beads that make up a colorful design. People place beads on strings and weave the strings together to create something that looks very similar to fabric. Native American craftspeople
10 count beads so that several different sizes may go together to make patterns for beadwork. The patterns are often **geometric** shapes, but sometimes they represent things from nature.

Modern craftspeople of many cultures use **manufactured** beads made of glass and plastic as well as natural stone and wood. The beads have numbers to
15 show their different sizes. Tiny beads may be size 22/0. This means that 22 of these beads will fit on 1 inch of string. Larger beads may be size 6/0, which means that 6 of these beads will fit on 1 inch of string.

Imagine that you want to make a piece of beadwork that is 12 inches square. How would you make this? First you would think of a design. Then you would
20 choose the colors and sizes of the beads. Finally, you would figure out how many beads you need.

For this example, the design will **comprise** 6 bands, or stripes, of equal **width** and different colors. The beads will be 6 different sizes: 20/0 white beads, 15/0 black beads, 12/0 green beads, 10/0 yellow beads, 8/0 blue beads, and 6/0 red
25 beads. Remember that the piece of beadwork will be 12 inches by 12 inches. This means that each of the 6 stripes will be 2 inches wide and 12 inches long. Each stripe will be made with one of these types of beads.

To find out how many beads you **require,** look at how many beads will cover 1 inch. Twenty white beads will cover 1 inch. Multiply 20 by 2 for the width and
30 20 by 12 for the length ($20 \times 2 = 40$; $20 \times 12 = 240$). Then multiply these two products ($40 \times 240 = 9,600$). You need 9,600 white beads. Use the same formula for the rest of the bead sizes. You will find that you need 5,400 black beads and 3,456 green beads. You also need 2,400 yellow beads, 1,536 blue beads, and 864 red beads. You need a total of 23,256 beads.

CONTENT CONNECTION

Beads are important in Native American culture. Native Americans have used beads as money, in dances, and in healing ceremonies for the sick. How is jewelry used in other cultures today? Hint: Think of jewelry that may be important at a wedding.

LANGUAGE CONNECTION

Beadwork is a compound word, or a word made from two words put together. In your own words, what does *beadwork* mean? Try to find other compound words in the article.

After You Read

A. Applying the Math

How many beads do you need to make a bookmark? Imagine that you are making a bookmark like the one below. It will be 4 inches tall and 2 inches wide. You are using 5 types of beads: 8/0 red beads, 8/0 green beads, 6/0 yellow beads, 4/0 blue beads, and 2/0 white beads. In the boxes that connect to the sections of the bookmark, show how to find the number of beads you need for each section. Then draw the beads in the outline of the bookmark below. Finally, add together the numbers from the third line of each box to find the total number of beads in the bookmark. Some have been done for you.

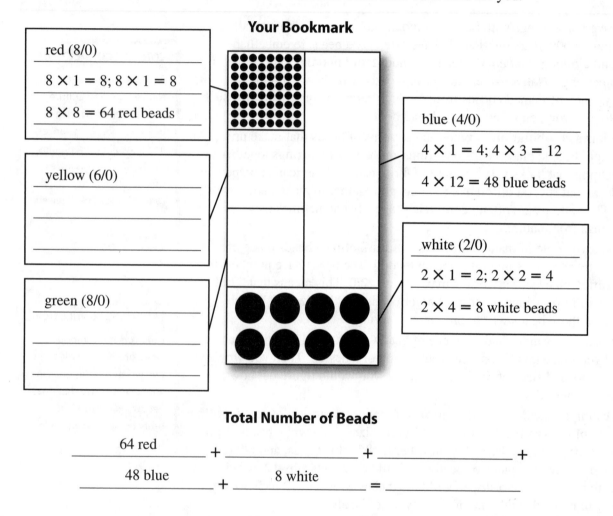

Your Bookmark

red (8/0)

$8 \times 1 = 8; 8 \times 1 = 8$

$8 \times 8 = 64$ red beads

yellow (6/0)

green (8/0)

blue (4/0)

$4 \times 1 = 4; 4 \times 3 = 12$

$4 \times 12 = 48$ blue beads

white (2/0)

$2 \times 1 = 2; 2 \times 2 = 4$

$2 \times 4 = 8$ white beads

Total Number of Beads

64 red _____ + _____ + _____ +

48 blue _____ + ____ 8 white ____ = _____

What did you learn about how to make beadwork? Write two or more sentences to answer this question. Did drawing the beads help you understand how math and beadwork are related? How?

_____

_____

_____

B. Comprehension Skills

Tip! **Think about how to find answers.** Think about what each sentence means. Try to say it to yourself in your own words before you complete it.

Mark box **a, b,** or **c** with an **X** before the choice that best completes each sentence.

Recalling Facts

1. *Embellish* means
   - ☐ **a.** "to grow in size."
   - ☐ **b.** "to make shiny and smooth."
   - ☐ **c.** "to add detail in order to decorate or improve something."

2. Twenty-two size 22/0 beads will fit
   - ☐ **a.** in a square.
   - ☐ **b.** across one 11-inch string.
   - ☐ **c.** on 1 inch of string.

3. The number of size 12/0 beads that will fit on a 12-inch string is
   - ☐ **a.** 24.
   - ☐ **b.** 48.
   - ☐ **c.** 144.

4. Beadwork is
   - ☐ **a.** material that beads are made from.
   - ☐ **b.** a combination of beads that make up a colorful design.
   - ☐ **c.** the process that people use to put beads on a string.

5. In the beadwork example in the article,
   - ☐ **a.** the 6/0 red beads are the largest of the beads.
   - ☐ **b.** the 20/0 white beads are the largest of the beads.
   - ☐ **c.** more 8/0 blue beads are needed than 20/0 white beads.

Understanding Ideas

1. From the article, you can conclude that
   - ☐ **a.** modern beadwork is more beautiful than ancient beadwork.
   - ☐ **b.** Native Americans used to make the beads in their beadwork.
   - ☐ **c.** Native Americans make nature designs more often than geometric designs.

2. The craft of beadwork
   - ☐ **a.** is 200 years old.
   - ☐ **b.** is thousands of years old.
   - ☐ **c.** is a modern craft.

3. To represent a mountain in a beadwork pattern, a person may use
   - ☐ **a.** a triangle.
   - ☐ **b.** a rectangle.
   - ☐ **c.** a slanted line.

4. Native Americans count beads to make their patterns
   - ☐ **a.** even.
   - ☐ **b.** all the same.
   - ☐ **c.** with many colors.

5. It is likely that Native Americans
   - ☐ **a.** invent patterns as they work.
   - ☐ **b.** work with beads to relax.
   - ☐ **c.** use a mathematical system to count beads.

C. Reading Strategies

1. Recognizing Words in Context

Find the word *represent* in the article. One definition below is closest to the meaning of that word. One definition has the opposite or nearly the opposite meaning. The remaining definition has a meaning that has nothing to do with the word. Label the definitions **C** for *closest*, **O** for *opposite* or *nearly opposite*, and **U** for *unrelated*.

_____ **a.** look taller than

_____ **b.** look completely different from

_____ **c.** look very similar to

2. Distinguishing Fact from Opinion

Two of the statements below present *facts*, which can be proved. The other statement is an *opinion*, which expresses someone's thoughts or beliefs. Label the statements **F** for *fact* and **O** for *opinion*.

_____ **a.** Native Americans use beads of many colors and sizes in their beadwork.

_____ **b.** Manufactured beads have numbers that show their sizes.

_____ **c.** Beadwork is the most difficult craft a person can do.

3. Making Correct Inferences

Two of the statements below are correct *inferences*, or reasonable guesses, that are based on information in the article. The other statement is an incorrect, or faulty, inference. Label the statements **C** for *correct* inference and **I** for *incorrect* inference.

_____ **a.** Native Americans invented manufactured beads to make their work easier.

_____ **b.** Native Americans used to make their beads from natural materials because those were the only materials available to them.

_____ **c.** Math helps craftspeople calculate the amounts of materials they need.

4. Understanding Main Ideas

One of the statements below expresses the main idea of the article. Another statement is too general, or too broad. The other explains only part of the article; it is too narrow. Label the statements **M** for *main idea*, **B** for *too broad*, and **N** for *too narrow*.

_____ **a.** Math has been helpful to Native American beadworkers throughout history.

_____ **b.** Native Americans may use different bead sizes within the same pattern.

_____ **c.** The art of beadwork is thousands of years old.

5. Responding to the Article

Complete the following sentences in your own words:

One of the things I did best while reading "Counting in Native American Beadwork" was

_____

I think that I did this well because _____

_____

D. Expanding Vocabulary

Content-Area Words

Read each item carefully. Write on the line the word or phrase that best completes each sentence.

1. Eva used a ruler to _____ the width of her hand.
   measure   cover   rub

2. Manufactured toys are made _____.
   well   in large amounts   by hand

3. The artist will include many _____ in the painting to add detail to it.
   small features   mistakes   animals

4. Squares, rectangles, and _____ are geometric shapes.
   lines   mountains   triangles

5. The color orange is a combination of _____.
   red   yellow   red and yellow

Academic English

In the article "Counting in Native American Beadwork," you learned that *comprise* means "to include" or "to be made of." *Comprise* can refer to the way beadwork is made of different types of beads. *Comprise* can also refer to other things that are made of different things, as in the following sentence.

  These books comprise the stories of three different authors.

Complete the sentence below.

1. A delicious meal may *comprise* _____

Now use the word *comprise* in a sentence of your own.

2. _____

You also learned that *require* means "to have a need for something." *Require* can also mean "to make it necessary for someone to do a certain thing," as in the following sentence.

  Teachers require their students to be on time for class.

Complete the sentence below.

3. An illness may *require* a person to _____

Now use the word *require* in two sentences of your own.

4. _____

5. _____

 Share your new sentences with a partner.

Before You Read

 Think about what you know. Read the lesson title above. What do you think the article will be about? When do you add or multiply other than in school?

Vocabulary

The content-area and academic English words below appear in "Adding and Multiplying Are Related." Read the definitions and the example sentences.

Content-Area Words

calculations (kal´kyə lā´shənz) mathematical steps taken to find an answer
Example: I made a few *calculations* to find the number of days until my birthday.

addition (ə dish´ən) the process used to add numbers into one amount
Example: Marco used *addition* to find the total cost of the shirt and the belt.

sum (sum) the amount that is the result of addition
Example: Add two numbers together to find their *sum*.

multiplication (mul´tə pli kā´shən) the process of adding a number to itself a certain number of times
Example: Kwan used *multiplication* to see that 3 times 4 equals 12.

product (prod´əkt) the amount that is the result of multiplication
Example: The *product* of 2 and 7 is 14.

Academic English

estimate (es´tə māt´) to make an inexact or rough calculation of something
Example: I *estimate* that three large pizzas will be enough for the party.

process (pros´es) a series of actions that lead to a certain result
Example: The *process* to join the soccer team includes tryouts and written permission from a parent.

Read again the example sentences that follow the content-area and academic English word definitions. With a partner, discuss the meanings of the words and sentences. Then make up a sentence of your own for each word.

 Now skim the article and look for other words that are new to you. Write each new word and its definition in the Personal Dictionary.

While You Read

 Think about why you read. Which do you find easier to do, addition or multiplication? Do you know how they are related? As you read, look for similarities and differences between addition and multiplication.

Adding & Multiplying Are Related

1 Mario's uncle, Tío Manuel, decided to replace the old floor tiles in his restaurant with new tiles. The new tiles were to be the same size as the old tiles, so he needed the same number of tiles. Tío Manuel asked Mario to figure out how many tiles he would need. Mario began to count the tiles. Because the
5 restaurant was very large and the floor had many tiles, he kept losing count.

Mario needed a better method. After he realized that each row had 24.5 tiles, he rounded this number up to 25 to make his **calculations** easier to do. He knew that the rounded number would allow him to **estimate** the number of tiles his uncle would need. Mario wrote down 25 plus 25 plus 25, and so on. For each of
10 the 20 rows of tile, Mario wrote down another 25. When he was finished, he used **addition** and saw that his uncle would need 500 tiles.

Because Tío Manuel wanted to check this number, he looked at the floor and counted the number of tiles in a row. Then he counted the number of rows. Tío Manuel multiplied 25 by 20, and he too found that he needed 500 tiles. He
15 praised Mario for his math skills. However, Mario was surprised that he and his uncle had found the same answer. He had found the **sum** of the tiles through the **process** of addition. His uncle had used **multiplication.** Tío Manuel explained that adding 25 together 20 times was the same as multiplying 25 by 20.

Mario decided to try to use multiplication. He counted the number of tiles in
20 one row along a side wall. Then he counted the number of rows. He counted 20 tiles and 25 rows. Mario wrote down 20 times 25 and used multiplication to find the answer. He was astonished that the answer was again 500, because he had calculated the answer in a different way from his uncle. Why did 25 times 20 and 20 times 25 have the same answer?

25 Tío Manuel explained that changing the order of the factors (the numbers that are multiplied) does not change the **product** (the multiplication result). He showed Mario that the same rule works for addition. He counted the tiles along one wall and then along another. He showed that the sum of 20 and 25 is the same as the sum of 25 and 20: 45. Changing the order of the addends (the
30 numbers that are added) does not change the sum (the addition result). This is because both addition and multiplication follow a mathematical law called the *commutative law.*

CONTENT CONNECTION

Mario rounded 24.5 up to 25, the next whole number. We can round numbers up or down to the nearest whole number. For example, we can round 50.1 down to 50, and we can round 27.7 up to 28. What whole number would you round 32.3 to? 32.8?

LANGUAGE CONNECTION

He was astonished in this context means "he didn't expect." What word in the third paragraph has a similar meaning to *astonished?*

After You Read

A. Applying the Math

How many ways can you use to find the number of tiles on a floor? Imagine that
you need to find the number of tiles on the bathroom floor grid below. Show two ways
to find the answer by addition and two ways to find the answer by multiplication.
Then count the tiles to check your answer. An example has been done for you.

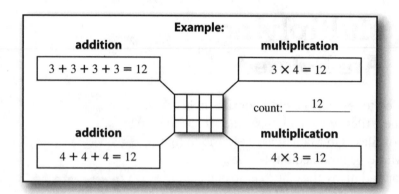

Example:

addition

$3 + 3 + 3 + 3 = 12$

multiplication

$3 \times 4 = 12$

count: _____12_____

addition

$4 + 4 + 4 = 12$

multiplication

$4 \times 3 = 12$

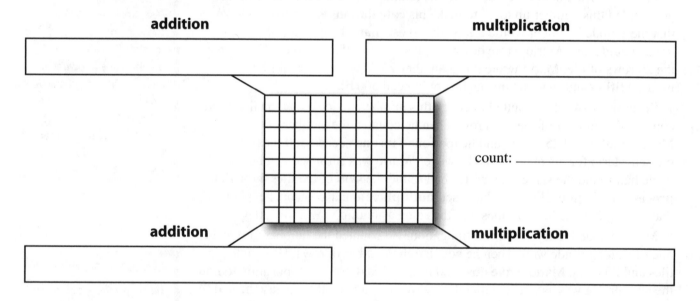

addition

multiplication

count: _____

addition

multiplication

Which method helped you find the number of tiles fastest—addition, multiplication,
or counting? Which method was slowest? Write two or more sentences to explain
your answers. How did this activity help you understand the connection between
addition and multiplication?

_____

_____

_____

B. Comprehension Skills

Tip! **Think about how to find answers.** Look back at different parts of the text. What facts help you figure out how to complete the sentences?

Mark box **a, b,** or **c** with an **X** before the choice that best completes each sentence.

Recalling Facts

1. Mario rounded up the number of tiles in each row to 25
   - ☐ **a.** to make the calculations easier to do.
   - ☐ **b.** to make sure that his uncle would have extra tiles.
   - ☐ **c.** to find the exact number of tiles.

2. Mario first determined that Tío Manuel would need 500 tiles by
   - ☐ **a.** addition.
   - ☐ **b.** subtraction.
   - ☐ **c.** multiplication.

3. Adding the number 25 to itself a total of 20 times is the same as
   - ☐ **a.** counting to 25.
   - ☐ **b.** adding 25 to 20.
   - ☐ **c.** multiplying 25 by 20.

4. The numbers that are multiplied and the multiplication result are
   - ☐ **a.** the factors and the sum.
   - ☐ **b.** the factors and the product.
   - ☐ **c.** the addends and the product.

5. The commutative law applies to
   - ☐ **a.** only addition.
   - ☐ **b.** only multiplication.
   - ☐ **c.** both addition and multiplication.

Understanding Ideas

1. The fastest way to figure out how many bricks are in a wall is probably to
   - ☐ **a.** use addition.
   - ☐ **b.** use multiplication.
   - ☐ **c.** count the bricks.

2. Mario and Tío Manuel's estimate of 500 tiles will probably provide
   - ☐ **a.** extra tiles.
   - ☐ **b.** not enough tiles.
   - ☐ **c.** the exact number of tiles that Tío Manuel needs.

3. An estimate is
   - ☐ **a.** an exact figure.
   - ☐ **b.** difficult to calculate.
   - ☐ **c.** close to the exact figure.

4. From the article, you can conclude that
   - ☐ **a.** addition is easier than multiplication.
   - ☐ **b.** multiplication is the same as addition.
   - ☐ **c.** addition and multiplication follow similar laws.

5. You can also conclude that the commutative law means that $a + b =$
   - ☐ **a.** $a \times b$.
   - ☐ **b.** $b + a$.
   - ☐ **c.** $b \times a$.

C. Reading Strategies

1. Recognizing Words in Context

Find the word *replace* in the article. One definition below is closest to the meaning of that word. One definition has the opposite or nearly the opposite meaning. The remaining definition has a meaning that has nothing to do with the word. Label the definitions **C** for *closest,* **O** for *opposite* or *nearly opposite,* and **U** for *unrelated.*

_____ **a.** leave something as it is

_____ **b.** imagine what something would look like

_____ **c.** take something away and provide something new

2. Distinguishing Fact from Opinion

Two of the statements below present *facts,* which can be proved. The other statement is an *opinion,* which expresses someone's thoughts or beliefs. Label the statements **F** for *fact* and **O** for *opinion.*

_____ **a.** Multiplication involves adding a number a certain number of times.

_____ **b.** The commutative law applies to addition.

_____ **c.** Addition is an easier process than multiplication.

3. Making Correct Inferences

Two of the statements below are correct *inferences,* or reasonable guesses, that are based on information in the article. The other statement is an incorrect, or faulty, inference. Label the statements **C** for *correct* inference and **I** for *incorrect* inference.

_____ **a.** Rounding a number can make addition and multiplication easier to do.

_____ **b.** The commutative law applies to all mathematical processes.

_____ **c.** In many situations, multiplication is faster than addition.

4. Understanding Main Ideas

One of the statements below expresses the main idea of the article. Another statement is too general, or too broad. The other explains only part of the article; it is too narrow. Label the statements **M** for *main idea,* **B** for *too broad,* and **N** for *too narrow.*

_____ **a.** Addition and multiplication follow similar laws and provide the same result for many math problems.

_____ **b.** The order of addends and factors does not affect the results of addition and multiplication problems.

_____ **c.** Addition and multiplication can help people solve many problems.

5. Responding to the Article

Complete the following sentence in your own words:

One thing in "Adding and Multiplying Are Related" that I cannot understand is

_____

_____

D. Expanding Vocabulary

Content-Area Words

Cross out one word in each row that is not related to the word in dark type.

1. calculations	steps	mathematics	count	answer
2. addition	remove	plus	sum	numbers
3. sum	addends	answer	addition	factors
4. multiplication	product	factors	times	subtract
5. product	numbers	angle	multiply	result

Academic English

In the article "Adding and Multiplying Are Related," you learned that *estimate* is a verb that means "to make an inexact or rough calculation of something." *Estimate* can also be a noun that means "a statement or document that provides an inexact guess of how much an amount of work or a service will cost," as in the following sentence.

The bakery gave us an estimate for the cost of a cake.

Complete the sentence below.

1. When Mari's car needed repairs, she got an *estimate* from _____

Now use the word *estimate* in a sentence of your own.

2. _____

_____

You also learned that *process* is a noun that means "a series of actions that lead to a certain result." *Process* can also be a verb that means "to handle by using a defined, usual set of steps," as in the following sentence.

The school will process students on the first day by asking them to fill out forms.

Complete the sentence below.

3. A step that a hospital takes to *process* sick patients is to ask for information about _____

Now use the word *process* in two sentences of your own.

4. _____

5. _____

 Share your new sentences with a partner.

Before You Read

Tip! **Think about what you know.** Read the title and the first sentence of the article on the opposite page. Think about what you already know about time. Is it the same time in other parts of the world as it is where you live?

Vocabulary

The content-area and academic English words below appear in "Worldwide Time Zones." Read the definitions and the example sentences.

Content-Area Words

zones (zōnz) areas or regions that are different from nearby areas in some way
Example: Signs often warn people not to enter construction *zones*.

longitude (lon′jə tōod′) distance on Earth's surface, measured in degrees east and west
Example: Airplane pilots use *longitude* lines to determine their location.

prime meridian (prīm mə rid′ē ən) the zero-degree line of longitude, which all other lines of longitude are measured from
Example: The time changes as people travel east or west from the *prime meridian*.

standardized (stan′dər dīzd′) caused things to use the same system
Example: Mr. Lin *standardized* the math tests, so they all contained similar problems.

daylight saving time (dā′līt′ sā′ving tīm) a period of time in which clocks are set one hour ahead to provide extra daylight during common work hours
Example: During *daylight saving time,* the Sun rises at an earlier time.

Academic English

accurately (ak′yər it lē) correctly
Example: She uses a dictionary to spell and pronounce words *accurately*.

adjust (ə just′) to change something in order to achieve a goal
Example: To make the room cooler, *adjust* the air conditioner.

Complete the sentences below that contain the content-area and academic English words above. Use the spaces provided. The first one has been done for you.

1. *Longitude* refers to a way to measure <u>distance</u>.

2. If the television is too loud, *adjust* the _____.

3. When *daylight saving time* occurs, people reset _____.

4. Joaquin solved the math problem *accurately,* so his answer was _____.

5. Two states that are in different time *zones* are California and _____.

6. The *prime meridian* is the line of longitude that measures _____.

7. The soccer league *standardized* its rules so that _____.

 Dictionary Now skim the article and look for other words that are new to you. Write each new word and its definition in the Personal Dictionary.

While You Read

Tip! **Think about why you read.** What do you already know about the different time zones around the world? Do you know why people created time zones? As you read, try to find the answer.

Worldwide Time Zones

1 Before the late 1800s, each town kept its own time. In some places, the town clockmaker was the person who kept the town clock set **accurately.** The clockmaker would watch the Sun until it reached its highest point in the sky. Then he would set the clock to noon. Because people set the time this way, the
5 time was slightly different in every town in the area.

When railroads came to the United States, train schedules (charts that show the times and places of each train stop) were confusing. Each stop was based on the time in that town. People needed a way to keep time that was consistent, or always the same, wherever they traveled.

10 In 1878 a Canadian, Sir Sandford Fleming, suggested that the world could be divided into 24 time **zones.** Each zone would be 15 degrees of **longitude** wide. Longitude lines are imaginary lines around Earth that pass through the North and South Poles.

In 1884 people from many countries met and made rules to set time around
15 the world. They decided that the line of longitude through Greenwich, England, would be the zero point of longitude, or zero degrees. They named this line the **prime meridian.** All of the other time zones in the world are measured from this point. That means that as a person moves west from the prime meridian, each time zone is one hour earlier. As a person moves east, each time zone is
20 one hour later.

Today all countries follow this system, but some countries have made changes to it. China is so large that it is in five time zones. However, the Chinese government decided to use only one zone. All Chinese citizens are on the same time. Russia is in 11 time zones, but 10 of them are one hour ahead of the time
25 they should follow according to their distance from the prime meridian.

In the United States, Congress **standardized** the time zones in 1918. It set the time zone lines so that the lines would not split up areas where many people lived. For this reason, the lines are not straight. The United States and its territories are in nine time zones. From east to west, these zones are the Eastern,
30 Central, Mountain, Pacific, Alaska, Hawaii-Aleutian, Samoan, Wake Island, and Guam time zones. This means that at 9:00 P.M. in New York City, it is noon on the island of Guam (9:00 P.M. − 9 hours = 0, or noon). Each year many states **adjust** their time zones to **daylight saving time.** This moves the time ahead one hour in March. These states go back to their regular time in November.

LANGUAGE CONNECTION

Notice how *clockmaker* contains the words *clock* and *maker*. It is a compound word (one word that is made from two words). Can you explain what a *clockmaker* is?

CONTENT CONNECTION

Imagine that you are in a time zone that is three time zones east of the prime meridian. If it is 8:00 A.M. at the prime meridian, what time is it in your time zone? What time would it be if you were three time zones west of the prime meridian?

After You Read

A. Organizing Ideas

What have you learned about time zones? Complete the outline below. Write down facts that you learned from the article. Some parts have been done for you.

Time Zones

I. Before time zones were created

   A. Each town kept its own time. _____

   B. _____

   C. _____

   D. Train schedules were confusing. _____

   E. _____

II. The creation of time zones

   A. _____

   B. _____

   C. In 1884 people met to make rules to set time around the world. ____

   D. _____

   E. _____

III. Time zones today

   A. All countries follow the time zone system, but some have made changes to it.

   B. _____

   C. Ten of Russia's 11 time zones are ahead by one hour.

   D. _____

   E. _____

What do you know about the creation of time zones? Write two or more sentences to answer this question. Did the outline help you answer the question? Why or why not?

_____

_____

_____

_____

B. Comprehension Skills

Tip! **Think about how to find answers.** Look back at what you read. The words in an answer are usually contained in a single sentence.

Mark box **a, b,** or **c** with an **X** before the choice that best completes each sentence.

Recalling Facts

1. Longitude lines are
   - ☐ **a.** any lines on a map.
   - ☐ **b.** imaginary lines around Earth.
   - ☐ **c.** the measure of daylight saving time.

2. Sir Sandford Fleming
   - ☐ **a.** invented daylight saving time.
   - ☐ **b.** was an English clockmaker.
   - ☐ **c.** suggested that Earth could be divided into time zones.

3. The prime meridian is
   - ☐ **a.** the zero point of longitude.
   - ☐ **b.** the last day of daylight saving time.
   - ☐ **c.** a system of 24 time zones.

4. China spreads across
   - ☐ **a.** three time zones.
   - ☐ **b.** five time zones.
   - ☐ **c.** nine time zones.

5. Russia spreads across
   - ☐ **a.** five time zones.
   - ☐ **b.** 11 time zones.
   - ☐ **c.** 10 time zones.

Understanding Ideas

1. When train schedules were based on the times in each town,
   - ☐ **a.** trains could never keep their schedules.
   - ☐ **b.** people in different towns did not communicate with each other.
   - ☐ **c.** a train might be scheduled to arrive at noon in two towns on the same day.

2. The world time zone system
   - ☐ **a.** has given people around the world a standard way to speak about time.
   - ☐ **b.** is not used by China or Russia.
   - ☐ **c.** will be replaced by a better system.

3. Congress did not set zone lines in areas where many people lived because
   - ☐ **a.** people wanted daylight saving time.
   - ☐ **b.** time zone lines are not straight.
   - ☐ **c.** it would be confusing for people to live near a border between zones.

4. Because the United States is west of the prime meridian,
   - ☐ **a.** it is east of Greenwich, England.
   - ☐ **b.** the time in New York is earlier than the time in Greenwich, England.
   - ☐ **c.** the time in New York is later than the time in Greenwich, England.

5. In the middle of the United States, the Sun rises
   - ☐ **a.** later than on the East Coast.
   - ☐ **b.** later than on the West Coast.
   - ☐ **c.** earlier than on the East Coast.

C. Reading Strategies

1. Recognizing Words in Context

Find the word *slightly* in the article. One definition below is closest to the meaning of that word. One definition has the opposite or nearly the opposite meaning. The remaining definition has a meaning that has nothing to do with the word. Label the definitions **C** for *closest*, **O** for *opposite* or *nearly opposite*, and **U** for *unrelated*.

_____ **a.** slowly

_____ **b.** a little bit

_____ **c.** greatly

2. Distinguishing Fact from Opinion

Two of the statements below present *facts,* which can be proved. The other statement is an *opinion,* which expresses someone's thoughts or beliefs. Label the statements **F** for *fact* and **O** for *opinion.*

_____ **a.** All time zones are measured from the prime meridian.

_____ **b.** Some countries do not follow the exact rules of the time zones.

_____ **c.** The Chinese government should use more than one time zone.

3. Making Correct Inferences

Two of the statements below are correct *inferences,* or reasonable guesses, that are based on information in the article. The other statement is an incorrect, or faulty, inference. Label the statements **C** for *correct* inference and **I** for *incorrect* inference.

_____ **a.** Sir Sandford Fleming suggested that people could use daylight saving time.

_____ **b.** Daylight saving time helps people spend less of the workday in the dark.

_____ **c.** The time is later on the East Coast of the United States than it is on the West Coast.

4. Understanding Main Ideas

One of the statements below expresses the main idea of the article. Another statement is too general, or too broad. The other explains only part of the article; it is too narrow. Label the statements **M** for *main idea,* **B** for *too broad,* and **N** for *too narrow.*

_____ **a.** People use the time zone system to keep time.

_____ **b.** Time zones provide a standard time system for people around the world.

_____ **c.** Each of the 24 time zones is 15 degrees of longitude wide.

5. Responding to the Article

Complete the following sentence in your own words:

What interested me most in "Worldwide Time Zones" was

_____

_____

D. Expanding Vocabulary

Content-Area Words

Complete each sentence with a word from the box. Write the missing word on the line.

zones	longitude	prime meridian	standardized	daylight saving time

1. We changed time _____ when we traveled from California to Florida.

2. We _____ our watches before the trip so that we would all have the same time.

3. Distance on Earth's surface may be measured in degrees of _____.

4. The time in a time zone is based on the zone's distance from the _____.

5. Tomorrow is the first day of _____, so don't forget to set the clocks ahead!

Academic English

In the article "Worldwide Time Zones," you learned that *accurately* means "correctly." *Accurately* can also mean "exactly" or "precisely," as in the following sentence.

   A thermometer should measure temperature accurately.

Complete the sentence below.

1. To measure his height *accurately,* Pablo used a _____

Now use the word *accurately* in a sentence of your own.

2. _____

_____

You also learned that *adjust* means "to change something in order to achieve a goal." *Adjust* can also mean "to adapt in order to become used to something," as in the following sentence.

   Rukmini found it difficult to adjust to city life after she had lived in the country.

Complete the sentence below.

3. Donnell needed to *adjust* to the cold weather when _____

Now use the word *adjust* in two sentences of your own.

4. _____

5. _____

 Talk It Over Share your new sentences with a partner.

Before You Read

 Think about what you know. Read the title and the first sentence of the article on the opposite page. What do you think the article will be about? How could math help you make a guess about the future?

Vocabulary

The content-area and academic English words below appear in "Statistics." Read the definitions and the example sentences.

Content-Area Words

percentage (pər sen′tij) a certain part of a whole expressed as parts out of every hundred
Example: What *percentage* of the students in our school play a sport?

formulas (fôr′myə ləz) mathematical ways to show a rule or solve a problem
Example: In math class, I learned *formulas* to calculate the areas of shapes.

engineers (en´ji nērz′) people who design and build structures or machines
Example: It takes many *engineers* to design and build a car.

analysis (ə nal′ə sis) a careful, detailed study of something
Example: The newspaper article provided an *analysis* of the new movie.

average (av′rij) the sum of a set of numbers divided by how many numbers are in the set
Example: Naomi found that the *average* of her classmates' heights was five feet.

Academic English

constant (kon′stənt) not changing
Example: The temperature stayed *constant* at 80 degrees Fahrenheit all day.

predicted (pri dikt′əd) used current knowledge to make a guess about the future
Example: When I saw the dark clouds, I *predicted* that it would rain.

Rate each vocabulary word according to the following scale. Write a number next to each content-area and academic English word.

4   I have never seen the word before.

3   I have seen the word but do not know what it means.

2   I know what the word means when I read it.

1   I use the word myself in speaking or writing.

 Now skim the article and look for other words that are new to you. Write each new word and its definition in the Personal Dictionary.

While You Read

Tip! **Think about why you read.** Statistics are useful in many different types of work. What type of work do you want to do someday? As you read, try to think of ways that statistics could help you do that type of work.

Statistics

1 Statistics is a type of mathematics that helps people calculate guesses when they do not have enough information. Doctors may use statistics to find the best cure for an illness. One way for them to do this is to treat a group of people with a new medicine. They count how many of these people get better. Then they can
5 calculate the **percentage** of people who would get better if they took that medicine. They compare the percentages from different medicines. Doctors can use statistics **formulas** and charts to decide which medicines work best.

Engineers who plan street systems often use statistics to help create the best designs to control traffic in an area. To find out whether they must change the
10 design of the streets, engineers look at how many people live in the area. They also look at how many people use the streets in the area. They have to figure out whether these numbers are likely to stay the same or whether they may change. An increase in the number of drivers may mean that engineers have to improve the design of area streets.

15 For example, statistics showed that the number of drivers in Maytown in 1970 was 30,400. By 1980 the number of drivers had risen to 33,500. This was about a 10-percent increase over 10 years ($33,500 - 30,400 = 3,100$; $3,100 \div 30,400 = 0.10$). In 1990 the number of drivers was 36,900, and in 2000 it was 41,000. The increase in drivers was **constant** at about 10 percent every 10 years. During
20 the same years, the job market, or the number and types of jobs people could get in Maytown, had grown at a steady rate. This market growth brought more and more people to Maytown. This meant that the percentage increase in drivers would probably remain steady.

Engineers used statistical **analysis** to figure out whether the streets would
25 be able to handle the amount of traffic in Maytown through the year 2030. The engineers **predicted** from the statistics that the number of drivers would continue to increase by 10 percent for each 10-year period from 2000 through 2030.

Statistics can also help a person choose the best product. Imagine that you want to find the batteries that last the longest for a handheld game. You visit
30 several Web sites. Each of these sites gives results from battery tests. However, the results do not completely agree. People may have run their tests in different ways, which could cause different results. In this case, you could find the **average** of the test results to decide which battery to use. Statistics is a mathematical tool that helps people make decisions.

LANGUAGE CONNECTION

Treat is a verb that means "to give medical attention to." *Treat* can also be a noun that means "something that gives pleasure," as in the sentence "Ice cream is a special treat." Which definition are you more familiar with?

CONTENT CONNECTION

Statistics are important in many sports. For example, every professional baseball player has a set of statistics, such as how often he hits the ball. Why would a coach want to know statistics about the players on his team or another team?

After You Read

A. Organizing Ideas

Who uses statistics to solve problems? Complete the chart below. In each circle, write down one type of person from the article who may use statistics. Then write at least two sentences about how statistics could help that person make a decision or solve a problem. In the square, write down an idea of your own about how statistics could help someone else. Some have been done for you.

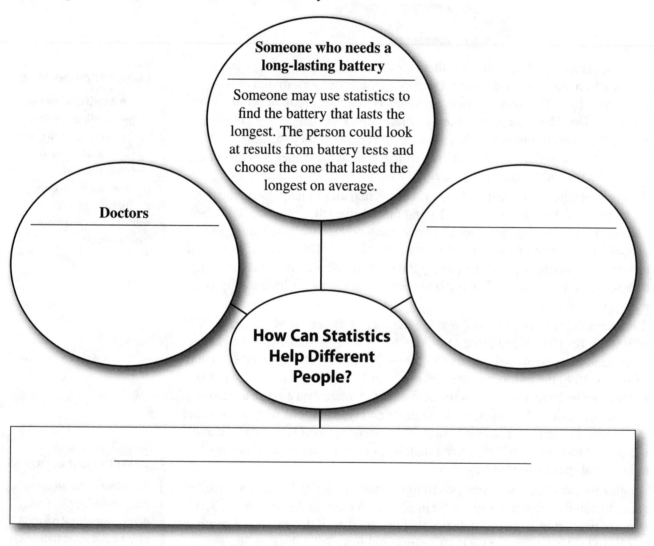

What is one way that statistics could help you make a decision or solve a problem? Write two or more sentences to answer this question. Did the chart help you understand different ways that statistics could be useful? Explain your answer.

_____

_____

B. Comprehension Skills

Tip! **Think about how to find answers.** Read each sentence below. Underline the words that will help you figure out how to complete each item.

Mark box **a, b,** or **c** with an **X** before the choice that best completes each sentence.

Recalling Facts

1. Statistics is a type of mathematics that helps people
   - ☐ **a.** find percentages.
   - ☐ **b.** calculate guesses.
   - ☐ **c.** find the best medicines.

2. The number of drivers in Maytown between 1970 and 1980
   - ☐ **a.** increased.
   - ☐ **b.** decreased.
   - ☐ **c.** stayed the same.

3. The job market in Maytown
   - ☐ **a.** had not changed in recent years.
   - ☐ **b.** had decreased at a steady rate.
   - ☐ **c.** had grown at a steady rate.

4. Engineers had to figure out whether the Maytown streets could handle traffic
   - ☐ **a.** through the year 2010.
   - ☐ **b.** through the year 2020.
   - ☐ **c.** through the year 2030.

5. In the battery test example, an average was needed because
   - ☐ **a.** the results did not agree.
   - ☐ **b.** all of the results were wrong.
   - ☐ **c.** it was not clear where the results came from.

Understanding Ideas

1. From the article, you can conclude that statistics
   - ☐ **a.** can be useful to anyone.
   - ☐ **b.** are important only in science.
   - ☐ **c.** are used only by professionals.

2. A teacher may use statistics
   - ☐ **a.** to spell a word correctly.
   - ☐ **b.** to count the students in a class.
   - ☐ **c.** to compare the progress of students in a class.

3. It is likely that statistics
   - ☐ **a.** help people make decisions.
   - ☐ **b.** do not help people find averages.
   - ☐ **c.** help people find any answer that involves numbers.

4. An increase in the number of drivers may mean that engineers have to redesign the Maytown streets because
   - ☐ **a.** the streets are in poor condition.
   - ☐ **b.** the streets are designed for a smaller number of drivers.
   - ☐ **c.** people will move away if the streets are not redesigned.

5. It would not make sense to find the average of statistics from
   - ☐ **a.** similar events.
   - ☐ **b.** completely different events.
   - ☐ **c.** the same event in different years.

C. Reading Strategies

1. Recognizing Words in Context

Find the word *steady* in the article. One definition below is closest to the meaning of that word. One definition has the opposite or nearly the opposite meaning. The remaining definition has a meaning that has nothing to do with the word. Label the definitions **C** for *closest*, **O** for *opposite* or *nearly opposite*, and **U** for *unrelated*.

_____ **a.** regular

_____ **b.** changing often

_____ **c.** caring

2. Distinguishing Fact from Opinion

Two of the statements below present *facts,* which can be proved. The other statement is an *opinion,* which expresses someone's thoughts or beliefs. Label the statements **F** for *fact* and **O** for *opinion.*

_____ **a.** Statistics can help doctors determine the best cure for an illness.

_____ **b.** Statistics is a difficult type of mathematics.

_____ **c.** An average is a number that represents a set of numbers.

3. Making Correct Inferences

Two of the statements below are correct *inferences,* or reasonable guesses, that are based on information in the article. The other statement is an incorrect, or faulty, inference. Label the statements **C** for *correct* inference and **I** for *incorrect* inference.

_____ **a.** Statistics often requires a person to collect many numbers related to a subject.

_____ **b.** People may use statistics about the past to make decisions about the future.

_____ **c.** Guesses based on statistics are always correct.

4. Understanding Main Ideas

One of the statements below expresses the main idea of the article. Another statement is too general, or too broad. The other explains only part of the article; it is too narrow. Label the statements **M** for *main idea,* **B** for *too broad,* and **N** for *too narrow.*

_____ **a.** Engineers may use statistics to make decisions about the way they build things.

_____ **b.** Statistics can help people make decisions based on past information.

_____ **c.** Statistics is a type of mathematics.

5. Responding to the Article

Complete the following sentence in your own words:

From reading "Statistics," I have learned

_____

_____

D. Expanding Vocabulary

Content-Area Words

Read each item carefully. Write on the line the word or phrase that best completes
each sentence.

1. The doctor must _____ before she can do an analysis of his health.
   examine him   read a book   greet him

2. A group of engineers will _____ in our town.
   elect new leaders   build a new bridge   rename the library

3. A person must know how to add and _____ to calculate an average.
   multiply   subtract   divide

4. To _____, I will use the formulas we learned in math class.
   solve these problems   write better   learn to dance

5. She got a large percentage of votes and _____ the election.
   lost   won   forgot about

Academic English

In the article "Statistics," you learned that *constant* means "not changing." *Constant*
can also mean "continuing without stopping," as in the following sentence.

   We have had constant sunshine today.

Complete the sentence below.

1. I tried to study, but I was bothered by the *constant* sound of _____

Now use the word *constant* in a sentence of your own.

2. _____

You also learned that *predicted* means "used current knowledge to make a guess about
the future." *Predicted* can relate to the use of statistics to make a guess about the
future. *Predicted* can also relate to other guesses about the future, as in the following
sentence.

   Adji predicted that he would receive an A on his math test.

Complete the sentence below.

3. The soccer coach *predicted* that his team would _____

Now use the word *predicted* in two sentences of your own.

4. _____

5. _____

 Share your new sentences with a partner.

Before You Read

 Think about what you know. Read the title and the first sentence of the article on the opposite page. What do you already know about newspapers and the advertisements inside them?

Vocabulary

The content-area and academic English words below appear in "Newspaper Circulation and Revenue." Read the definitions and the example sentences.

Content-Area Words

advertising (ad′vər tī′zing) information about a product that is given to the public
> *Example:* Companies buy *advertising* space on signs, in newspapers, and on television.

circulation (sur′kyə lā′shən) the total number of copies that a newspaper sells each day
> *Example:* Interesting stories may increase the *circulation* of a newspaper.

revenue (rev′ə nōō′) the amount of money that a company makes
> *Example:* The *revenue* of a grocery store comes from the sale of food products.

market share (mär′kit shār) the percentage of total sales that one company holds for a product or service
> *Example:* Because Mario's bakery is the only one in town, its *market share* is 100 percent.

charge (chärj) to ask as the price of a service or product
> *Example:* The new restaurant will *charge* $4 for a sandwich.

Academic English

justify (jus′tə fī′) to show something to be a good decision
> *Example:* I cannot *justify* why I watched a movie when I had homework to do.

expand (iks pand′) to make larger in size or amount
> *Example:* To *expand* my knowledge of history, I read a book about World War I.

Answer the questions below. Circle the part of each question that is the answer. The first one has been done for you.

1. Is *revenue* (money that a company earns) or money that a company spends?
2. When stores *charge* people for bags of ice, do people pay money or take money?
3. When balloons *expand*, do they become bigger or smaller?
4. If a newspaper has a low *circulation*, did many people or few people buy it?
5. Is it easier for people to *justify* the purchase of things they need or things they do not need?
6. Would a company buy *advertising* space to learn about a product or to tell others about a product?
7. If a company has a high *market share*, is it successful or unsuccessful?

 Now skim the article and look for other words that are new to you. Write each new word and its definition in the Personal Dictionary.

While You Read

Tip! **Think about why you read.** Newspapers need both readers and advertising in order to be successful. Which of these brings newspapers more money? As you read, try to find the answer.

Newspaper Circulation and Revenue

1 Newspaper companies make money in two ways: they sell papers and they sell **advertising** space. **Circulation** is the total number of copies that a newspaper sells each day. For most newspapers, the sale of papers makes up about 18 percent of the total **revenue.** Revenue is the money that a company
5 makes. The rest of the revenue comes from the sale of advertising.

Besides its own circulation, a newspaper must look at its **market share.** Market share for a daily city newspaper has to do with how many papers it sells compared to how many papers are sold by other daily newspaper companies in that city. A newspaper's market share also involves how much money people
10 spend to advertise in that paper compared to how much people spend to advertise in other newspapers.

People usually express advertising market share as a percentage. For example, the *Boston Globe* holds an 85-percent share of newspaper advertising revenue in Boston. This means that 85 percent of the newspaper advertising that companies
15 buy in Boston is in the *Globe*.

The greater the circulation a newspaper has, the more it can **charge** for advertising. The amount that an advertiser pays for advertising space, or ad space, in a newspaper is based on the number of people who read the paper. If a newspaper has a large circulation, many readers will see the advertising in the
20 paper. That newspaper can charge more for ad space than a paper with a smaller circulation can. If paying a higher price means more people will see an ad, an advertiser often can **justify** the higher cost for ad space.

Imagine this example. The *Daily Times* has a circulation of 25,000 readers. It charges $1,500 for an ad that takes up ¼ of a page. The *Gazette* has a
25 circulation of 35,000. It charges $1,750 for a ¼-page ad. An ad in the *Gazette* costs more, but the *Gazette* is the better value because more people read it. The proof is in the math. The advertiser can divide the cost of the ad by the number of readers to figure out the cost per reader. The *Times* charges $.06 per reader ($1,500 ÷ 25,000 = $.06). The *Gazette* charges $.05 per reader ($1,750 ÷
30 35,000 = $.05). Even though a ¼-page ad costs more in the *Gazette*, the advertiser is paying less per reader.

Newspapers try to find out the kinds of things that readers like or do not like in a newspaper. With this information, the newspaper can make changes to the paper to help **expand** its circulation. As circulation increases, the newspaper
35 earns more money because it sells more papers. It can also charge more for ad space. An increase in circulation is a "can't lose" situation.

LANGUAGE CONNECTION

Many English words have more than one meaning. The word *rest* in line 5 means "the amount that remains." What is another meaning for the word *rest*?

CONTENT CONNECTION

Many businesses advertise their products or services in a number of different places. Some businesses advertise not only in newspapers, but also on television, on the radio, on the Internet, and on signs. What are some advertisements that you have seen or heard recently?

After You Read

A. Applying the Math

How would you spend money on advertising? Imagine that you are opening a new restaurant. You have $10,000 to spend on advertising in newspapers. Use the information below to decide which newspapers to advertise in, how many ads to buy, and what size ads to use. Be sure to stay within your budget. An example has been done for you.

The *Courier*
Circulation: 10,000 readers daily

¼ page $1,500	¼ page $1,500	full page $3,000
½ page $2,000		

The *Times*
Circulation: 20,000 readers daily

¼ page $2,000	¼ page $2,000	full page $5,000
½ page $4,000		

Advertising Plan
Budget: $10,000

Newspaper	Size of Ad	Cost per Ad	Cost per Reader	Number of Ads	Total Cost
Example: *Courier*	¼ page	$1,500	$1,500 ÷ 10,000 = $0.15	2	$3,000

What are the reasons for your choices? What did you learn about the way advertisers decide how to spend their money? Write two or more sentences to answer these questions. When could you use this type of chart again?

_____

_____

_____

B. Comprehension Skills

 Think about how to find answers. Look back at what you read. The information is in the text, but you may have to look in several sentences to find it.

Mark box **a, b,** or **c** with an **X** before the choice that best completes each sentence.

Recalling Facts

1. Circulation is the
   - ☐ **a.** market share of a company.
   - ☐ **b.** cost per reader for ad space.
   - ☐ **c.** number of newspapers sold each day.

2. About 18 percent of a newspaper's total revenue comes from
   - ☐ **a.** the sale of papers.
   - ☐ **b.** its market share.
   - ☐ **c.** the sale of ad space.

3. A newspaper company earns money when it
   - ☐ **a.** studies market share.
   - ☐ **b.** sells ad space.
   - ☐ **c.** sells newspapers and ad space.

4. Because the *Gazette* has more readers than the *Daily Times* does, the *Gazette*
   - ☐ **a.** is a better newspaper.
   - ☐ **b.** is a better value for advertisers.
   - ☐ **c.** earns less advertising revenue.

5. It is not true that newspapers
   - ☐ **a.** want to know what readers like or dislike about their newspaper.
   - ☐ **b.** charge for ad space based on circulation.
   - ☐ **c.** express circulation as a percentage.

Understanding Ideas

1. The advertising market share of a newspaper company is based on
   - ☐ **a.** the cost of ad space.
   - ☐ **b.** the money the newspaper earns.
   - ☐ **c.** the size of the ads in the paper.

2. The people who calculate newspaper sales would need to know how many people
   - ☐ **a.** buy the Sunday paper.
   - ☐ **b.** work for the newspaper.
   - ☐ **c.** watch the news on television.

3. A large newspaper can charge more for ad space than a small newspaper can because the large newspaper
   - ☐ **a.** charges less for the paper.
   - ☐ **b.** has more readers.
   - ☐ **c.** knows more about its readers.

4. A good way for a newspaper to increase its advertising market share is to
   - ☐ **a.** increase its amount of ad space.
   - ☐ **b.** charge more for ad space.
   - ☐ **c.** increase its circulation.

5. The circulation of a newspaper is important to advertisers because it shows
   - ☐ **a.** how many people see the ads.
   - ☐ **b.** how the newspaper earns money.
   - ☐ **c.** how much ad space is available.

C. Reading Strategies

1. Recognizing Words in Context

Find the word *express* in the article. One definition below is closest to the meaning of that word. One definition has the opposite or nearly the opposite meaning. The remaining definition has a meaning that has nothing to do with the word. Label the definitions **C** for *closest*, **O** for *opposite* or *nearly opposite*, and **U** for *unrelated*.

_____ **a.** dislike

_____ **b.** display

_____ **c.** do not show

2. Distinguishing Fact from Opinion

Two of the statements below present *facts,* which can be proved. The other statement is an *opinion,* which expresses someone's thoughts or beliefs. Label the statements **F** for *fact* and **O** for *opinion.*

_____ **a.** A newspaper's circulation determines how much it can charge for ad space.

_____ **b.** Paper sales make up about 18 percent of newspaper earnings.

_____ **c.** Advertisers should place ads only in newspapers with large circulations.

3. Making Correct Inferences

Two of the statements below are correct *inferences,* or reasonable guesses, that are based on information in the article. The other statement is an incorrect, or faulty, inference. Label the statements **C** for *correct* inference and **I** for *incorrect* inference.

_____ **a.** Advertisers want to increase the sales of their products.

_____ **b.** A newspaper company does not need to pay attention to its market share if the paper has a large circulation.

_____ **c.** Circulation is important for revenue from both paper sales and ad sales.

4. Understanding Main Ideas

One of the statements below expresses the main idea of the article. Another statement is too general, or too broad. The other explains only part of the article; it is too narrow. Label the statements **M** for *main idea,* **B** for *too broad,* and **N** for *too narrow.*

_____ **a.** Newspaper companies make money in different ways.

_____ **b.** Newspapers with many readers can charge high prices for ad space.

_____ **c.** Newspapers make money from the sales of papers and ad space.

5. Responding to the Article

Complete the following sentence in your own words:

Before reading "Newspaper Circulation and Revenue," I already knew

_____

_____

D. Expanding Vocabulary

Content-Area Words

Complete each analogy with a word from the box. Write the missing word on the line.

| advertising | circulation | revenue | market share | charge |

1. prize : win :: _____ : earn

2. percentage : whole :: _____ : total

3. attendance : play :: _____ : newspaper

4. pay : customer :: _____ : seller

5. book : subject :: _____ : product

Academic English

In the article "Newspaper Circulation and Revenue," you learned that *justify* means "to show something to be a good decision." *Justify* can relate to a decision to spend more money to place ads in a newspaper with a large circulation. *Justify* can also relate to other decisions that people show to be good, as in the following sentence.

Because I have not eaten sweets all week, I can justify eating dessert tonight.

Complete the sentence below.

1. Nari can *justify* her decision to stay up late because _____

Now use the word *justify* in a sentence of your own.

2. _____

_____

You also learned that *expand* means "to make larger in size or amount." *Expand* can also mean "to discuss or explain in more detail," as in the following sentence.

The teacher asked me to expand on my answer by adding details.

Complete the sentence below.

3. Their book reports *expand* on different parts of the book, such as _____

Now use the word *expand* in two sentences of your own.

4. _____

5. _____

 Share your new sentences with a partner.

Writing a Journal Entry

Read the journal entry. Then complete the sentences. Use words from the Word Bank.

Word Bank

combination   predicted
constant   require
charged

July 22

Dear Journal,

Today I went to a scuba diving lesson with my friend Suwon! Diving companies

(1) _____ divers to take lessons before they go into the water.

During the lesson, we learned how to put on a (2) _____ of items,

such as rubber suits, goggles, and tanks that provide a (3) _____

supply of oxygen to breathe. I (4) _____ that I would be afraid to go

underwater, but it was actually a lot of fun. The company (5) _____

$100 for the lesson, but it was worth it. I hope to scuba dive in the ocean

someday!

Kaya

Reading an E-mail

Read the e-mail. Circle the word that completes each sentence.

INSTA-CHAT

Dear Vadim,

I am back from Australia! The airplane crossed several time (**zones, formulas**) during the trip, so I had to (**advertise, adjust**) my watch to the correct time. It took a while to remember the (**analysis, calculations**) I needed to make to figure out the time, because I haven't been in school all summer. Also, I was tired—the trip from Australia was a long (**product, process**). I can (**justify, standardize**) resting all day today!

Your friend,

Anita

Work with a partner. Talk about what the words mean. How can you use the words to talk about a newspaper? List your ideas in the outline of the newspaper below.

detail	width	percentage	circulation	revenue
comprise	estimate	accurately	sum	expand

Use all of the words above in complete sentences of your own. Each sentence may include one or more of the words. To help you start writing, look at the ideas you wrote about. After you write your sentences, read them over. If you find a mistake, correct it.

_____

_____

_____

_____

_____

_____

Before You Read

 Think about what you know. Skim the article on the opposite page. Have you ever noticed that people measure things differently in different countries? What amounts would you use to describe the size of a room in the United States?

Vocabulary

The content-area and academic English words below appear in "The Japanese Tatami Measurement." Read the definitions and the example sentences.

Content-Area Words

unit (ū′nit) a set amount of something used to measure other amounts of the same thing
  Example: An hour is a *unit* of time.

measurement (mezh′ər mənt) the process of finding the exact size or amount of something
  Example: A ruler is a tool that people use for *measurement*.

accommodate (ə kom′ə dāt′) to have enough room for a certain number of people or things
  Example: Our school dining hall can *accommodate* more than 400 students.

fortune (fôr′chən) the luck of a person, whether good or bad
  Example: I had the good *fortune* to get home before the storm began.

grid (grid) a pattern made of many lines that cross to form squares
  Example: This city map shows that the straight streets form a *grid*.

Academic English

culture (kul′chər) the arts, beliefs, and customs of a certain group of people
  Example: Freedom of speech is an important part of American *culture*.

ensure (en shoor′) to make sure or certain of something
  Example: Her snow boots *ensure* that her feet stay dry in winter.

Answer the questions below about the content-area and academic English words. Write your answers in the spaces provided. The first one has been done for you.

1. What word goes with *have a lucky day?* _____fortune_____

2. What word goes with *figure out how big something is?* _____

3. What word goes with *the clothing and music of a group of people?* _____

4. What word goes with *lines that form squares?* _____

5. What word goes with *an amount used to measure something?* _____

6. What word goes with *to have enough space for 12 people?* _____

7. What word goes with *to check that doors are locked?* _____

 Now skim the article and look for other words that are new to you. Write each new word and its definition in the Personal Dictionary.

While You Read

Tip! **Think about why you read.** Did you know that people in the Japanese culture measure rooms by the size of floor mats called *tatami?* Write down a question about the tatami measurement that you would like to know the answer to. As you read, try to find the answer.

The Japanese Tatami Measurement

1 Japanese **culture** is different from American culture in some ways. One difference involves the houses where people live. American homes have solid walls, and carpets often cover the floors. Japanese homes often use paper screens and sliding doors as walls, and straw mats may cover the floors.

5 The straw mats are called *tatami.* The tatami mat has been a part of Japanese culture for more than 1,000 years. At first only rich people used them. As time went on, more and more people began to use them. Eventually almost everyone in Japan used tatami mats. Today many Japanese people choose tatami floors instead of carpeting or bare floors.

10 A true tatami mat has three parts: a soft reed cover, straw filling, and cloth around the edges. Tatami makers use strong thread to sew the parts together so that the mats keep their shape. Because regular shoes can damage tatami, many Japanese people wear split-toe socks called *tabi* when they are indoors. Scientific tests show that tatami mats work well in the humid climate of Japan,
15 because they take in moisture, or wetness, from the air.

In Japan, people describe the size of a room as the number of tatami mats that can fit on the floor inside the room. *Jo* is a Japanese **unit** of **measurement** that is equal to the area of a tatami mat, which is usually about 90 centimeters by 180 centimeters (about 3 feet by 6 feet). A 20-jo room is equal to the area of 20 mats
20 and can **accommodate** 20 adults who are sitting together. A room that is 6 jo would be a room of average size.

Tatami mats come in different shapes and sizes. In one part of Japan, tatami mats may be 3 feet by 6 feet. In another part, they may be 5 feet by 8 feet. This means that a 6-jo room in some buildings may be smaller than a 6-jo room in
25 other buildings. The size of a jo depends on where a person lives.

According to the Chinese belief of *feng shui*, the position of furniture in the home can affect the **fortune** of the owner. In a similar way, some Japanese people believe that the number and pattern of tatami mats can bring good or bad fortune to a household. Some people think that mats that are arranged on the
30 floor in a **grid** pattern will bring bad luck. Others believe that a room size of five and a half tatami mats will **ensure** good fortune.

LANGUAGE CONNECTION

Do you know what the word *humid* means? Look at the words around it. Then write down what you think *humid* means. Share your definition with a partner.

CONTENT CONNECTION

Feng shui involves the placement of furniture in harmony with nature. Some believe that good feng shui helps a person feel peaceful.

After You Read

A. Applying the Math

How does the tatami measurement compare to measurement in feet? Use the space below to draw the floor of a 6-jo room in a Japanese home. The floor should be covered with six tatami mats that are each 3 feet by 6 feet. First draw the floor of the room. Label the sides of each mat with their sizes in feet. Then fill in the blanks below to show the size of the room in different units.

Width of one tatami mat: 3 feet _____

Length of one tatami mat: _____

Size of room in jo: _____

Length of room in feet: _____

Width of room in feet: _____

What did you learn about measurements in jo compared with measurements in feet? Which measurement do you prefer? Write two or more sentences to answer these questions. Did drawing the room help you understand the article? How?

_____

_____

_____

B. Comprehension Skills

Tip! **Think about how to find answers.** Read each sentence below. Underline the words that will help you figure out how to complete each item.

Mark box **a, b,** or **c** with an **X** before the choice that best completes each sentence.

Recalling Facts

1. A true tatami mat has
   - ☐ **a.** two parts.
   - ☐ **b.** three parts.
   - ☐ **c.** four parts.

2. It is not true that
   - ☐ **a.** a tatami mat is made of rice paper.
   - ☐ **b.** a true tatami mat has several parts.
   - ☐ **c.** people have used tatami mats for more than 1,000 years.

3. Jo is a Japanese unit of measurement
   - ☐ **a.** for a room of average size.
   - ☐ **b.** equal to the area of a tatami mat.
   - ☐ **c.** equal to a room size of five and a half tatami mats.

4. A room that measures 6 jo
   - ☐ **a.** is very large.
   - ☐ **b.** can fit six tatami mats on the floor.
   - ☐ **c.** is 6 feet by 6 feet.

5. Feng shui is
   - ☐ **a.** the name for a room that can fit five and a half tatami mats.
   - ☐ **b.** a grid pattern that people use to arrange tatami mats.
   - ☐ **c.** a belief that the position of furniture affects a person's fortune.

Understanding Ideas

1. From the article, you can conclude that the reed cover on a tatami mat is probably
   - ☐ **a.** hard.
   - ☐ **b.** sturdy.
   - ☐ **c.** easy to remove.

2. If someone knows that a room measures 6 jo, that person knows
   - ☐ **a.** the exact shape of the room.
   - ☐ **b.** the general size of the room.
   - ☐ **c.** the number of patterns on the floor of the room.

3. A 3-jo room probably would be about
   - ☐ **a.** 6 feet by 9 feet.
   - ☐ **b.** 3 feet by 6 feet.
   - ☐ **c.** 9 feet by 18 feet.

4. One thing that some people probably would *not* do with tatami mats is
   - ☐ **a.** walk on them.
   - ☐ **b.** sleep on them.
   - ☐ **c.** arrange them in a grid pattern.

5. To bring good fortune, a person might
   - ☐ **a.** arrange tatami mats in a grid pattern.
   - ☐ **b.** arrange all tatami mats in the same direction.
   - ☐ **c.** have rooms that are the size of five and a half tatami mats.

C. Reading Strategies

1. Recognizing Words in Context

Find the word *damage* in the article. One definition below is closest to the meaning of that word. One definition has the opposite or nearly the opposite meaning. The remaining definition has a meaning that has nothing to do with the word. Label the definitions **C** for *closest*, **O** for *opposite* or *nearly opposite*, and **U** for *unrelated*.

_____ **a.** harm

_____ **b.** cover

_____ **c.** protect

2. Distinguishing Fact from Opinion

Two of the statements below present *facts*, which can be proved. The other statement is an *opinion*, which expresses someone's thoughts or beliefs. Label the statements **F** for *fact* and **O** for *opinion*.

_____ **a.** A Japanese person would be likely to describe the size of a room in jo.

_____ **b.** It is easier to measure the size of a room in jo than in feet.

_____ **c.** The size of a jo varies throughout Japan.

3. Making Correct Inferences

Two of the statements below are correct *inferences*, or reasonable guesses, that are based on information in the article. The other statement is an incorrect, or faulty, inference. Label the statements **C** for *correct* inference and **I** for *incorrect* inference.

_____ **a.** Most Japanese people would consider a 15-jo room to be large.

_____ **b.** Tatami mats would not work in climates that are not humid.

_____ **c.** The tatami measurement has changed over time.

4. Understanding Main Ideas

One of the statements below expresses the main idea of the article. Another statement is too general, or too broad. The other explains only part of the article; it is too narrow. Label the statements **M** for *main idea*, **B** for *too broad*, and **N** for *too narrow*.

_____ **a.** People in Japan often measure rooms in jo, a measurement based on the Japanese tatami mat.

_____ **b.** Some Japanese people believe that the way they arrange tatami mats can affect their fortune.

_____ **c.** People in different countries often use different systems of measurement.

5. Responding to the Article

Complete the following sentences in your own words:

One of the things I did best while reading "The Japanese Tatami Measurement" was

_____

I think that I did this well because _____

_____

D. Expanding Vocabulary

Content-Area Words

Cross out one word in each row that is not related to the word in dark type.

1. **unit**	measure	jo	place	amount
2. **measurement**	size	tatami	exact	culture
3. **accommodate**	weather	space	enough	room
4. **fortune**	luck	good	bad	time
5. **grid**	lines	waves	cross	squares

Academic English

In the article "The Japanese Tatami Measurement," you learned that *culture* means "the arts, beliefs, and customs of a certain group of people." *Culture* can also mean "knowledge of the arts" or "good taste and manners," as in the following sentence.

My mother says that people of culture read good books.

Complete the sentence below.

1. I knew that Mr. Romano was a man of *culture* because _____

Now use the word *culture* in a sentence of your own.

2. _____

_____

You also learned that *ensure* means "to make sure or certain of something." *Ensure* can relate to Japanese beliefs about ways to make sure of good fortune. *Ensure* can also relate to ways to make sure of other things, as in the following sentence.

Plenty of sunlight and rain ensure that the flowers will grow.

Complete the sentence below.

3. I left early for school to *ensure* that _____

Now use the word *ensure* in two sentences of your own.

4. _____

5. _____

 Share your new sentences with a partner.

Lesson 12
Discounts and Markups Make a Profit

Before You Read

Tip! **Think about what you know.** Read the title and the first paragraph of the article on the opposite page. What do you think the article will be about? Think about the prices of certain items that you buy.

Vocabulary

The content-area and academic English words below appear in "Discounts and Markups Make a Profit." Read the definitions and the example sentences.

Content-Area Words

trends (trendz) the general choices of a group of people at a certain time
Example: Ramón reads magazines to learn about new music *trends*.

unit price (ū′nit prīs) the price for one item
Example: Five shirts at a *unit price* of $5 would cost $25.

quantity (kwon′tə tē) the amount or number of something
Example: Many items are cheaper when people buy them in a large *quantity*.

discount (dis′kount′) an amount that is subtracted from a full price
Example: The store gave us a *discount* on the bike because it had a scratch on it.

markup (märk′up′) an amount that a seller adds to an item's price to make a profit
Example: The store owner put a high *markup* on the fine leather shoes.

Academic English

style (stīl) a particular type of fashion
Example: My grandparents still dress in the *style* of the 1970s.

contribute (kən trib′ūt) to help to bring about a specific result
Example: All of the soccer players *contribute* to the success of the team.

Complete the sentences below that contain the content-area and academic English words above. Use the spaces provided. The first one has been done for you.

1. She enjoys health *trends* such as <u>new diet plans</u> .

2. After a meal, I *contribute* to the cleanup when I _____ .

3. My favorite shoe *style* is _____ .

4. If an item in a store has a *discount*, it is _____ .

5. My neighbor had a party and ordered a large *quantity* of _____ .

6. Stores add a *markup* to the price of items in order to _____ .

7. A usual *unit price* for a music CD would be _____ .

 Now skim the article and look for other words that are new to you. Write each new word and its definition in the Personal Dictionary.

While You Read

Tip! **Think about why you read.** If you owned a store, how would you decide the price of each item? What must stores consider when they calculate prices? As you read, try to answer this question.

Discounts and Markups Make a Profit

1 Claire is the buyer for Top-Mart store for women. The buyer is the person who decides what a store will sell and orders it. Claire has studied popular fashion **trends** and wants to buy spring purses and other items for the next year. She is working with her team to plan how many items to order. She and her
5 team will also decide how to price the items so that Top-Mart makes money.

Top-Mart has 100 stores across the country. Based on past sales, the supplier charges Top-Mart a **unit price** of $10 per purse. Claire and her team estimate that Top-Mart will sell about 7,500 purses. At that **quantity,** Claire knows that she can get a 5-percent **discount** from the supplier, because her order will be
10 more than $50,000. She multiplies $10 by .05 to find the discount of $0.50. Each purse will cost $9.50 ($10 − $0.50 = $9.50). Claire will spend $71,250 for the 7,500 purses she buys ($9.50 × 7,500 = $71,250).

After Claire orders the purses, the team figures the **markup** to set the price that Top-Mart will charge for each purse. The markup covers operating costs and
15 profit. Operating costs are expenses that Top-Mart has, such as wages, rent, and advertising. These costs are divided among the markups on all of the goods that Top-Mart sells. The operating cost markup is 20 percent. The profit markup is 30 percent. This means that the total markup has to be at least 50 percent. The company considers this the minimum markup. Claire and her team calculate that
20 a 50-percent markup on each purse would be $4.75 ($9.50 × 0.5 = $4.75). That would make the retail price, or the price in the store, $14.25.

The team thinks that the unique **style** of the purses will make people willing to buy them for more than $14.25. They decide that the retail price should be $15.99. This would mean a profit of 48.3 percent instead of 30 percent. How do
25 they calculate this percentage? First they subtract their cost from the retail price to find the profit for each purse ($15.99 − $9.50 = $6.49). Then they divide this amount by their cost for each purse ($6.49 ÷ $9.50 = 0.683, or 68.3 percent). Finally they subtract the operating cost markup of 20 percent.

Claire and her team figure out what the extra profit would mean. With the
30 regular markup, Top-Mart would earn a profit of $2.85 per purse ($9.50 × 0.3 = $2.85). That would be a profit of $21,375 if people buy all of the purses. At the higher markup, the total profit would be $34,413.75. With the higher markup, Claire and her team would help Top-Mart make an extra $13,038.75 in profit. Discounts and markups can help Claire and her team **contribute** to the success
35 of their store.

After You Read

A. Organizing Ideas

How do stores set their prices? Complete the chart below. In each box, write down one price that the purse in the article had at a certain point. Then write two or more sentences to explain who set the price and how they calculated it. Some have been done for you.

The Price of a Purse at Top-Mart

Price: _____$10_____ This is the price that the supplier charges per purse. The supplier sets this amount based on past sales.

↓

Price: _____$9.50_____ _____

↓

Price: _____ This is the retail price that Top-Mart would charge with the regular markup. The regular markup is made up of

↓

Price: _____ _____

What are some things that could have caused the final retail price to be lower? What could have caused it to be higher? Write two or more sentences to answer these questions. Did the chart help you understand how stores set their prices? How?

_____

_____

_____

B. Comprehension Skills

Tip! **Think about how to find answers.** Look back at what you read. The words in an answer are usually contained in a single sentence.

Mark box **a, b,** or **c** with an **X** before the choice that best completes each sentence.

Recalling Facts

1. The cost of each purse before the markup is
   - ☐ **a.** $9.50.
   - ☐ **b.** $10.
   - ☐ **c.** $15.99.

2. The markup includes
   - ☐ **a.** wages and rent.
   - ☐ **b.** retail price plus profit.
   - ☐ **c.** profit and operating costs.

3. After the markup of 50 percent, the retail price of the purse is
   - ☐ **a.** $9.50.
   - ☐ **b.** $14.25.
   - ☐ **c.** $15.99.

4. Wages, rent, and advertising are all examples of
   - ☐ **a.** operating costs.
   - ☐ **b.** profit markups.
   - ☐ **c.** operating discounts.

5. Claire and her team raise the retail price in order to
   - ☐ **a.** sell more purses.
   - ☐ **b.** give customers a discount.
   - ☐ **c.** increase the profit for Top-Mart.

Understanding Ideas

1. From the article, you can conclude that
   - ☐ **a.** stores charge too much for purses.
   - ☐ **b.** some stores have no operating costs.
   - ☐ **c.** if stores buy items at a discount, they can make a higher profit.

2. Large stores may offer lower prices than small stores do because large stores
   - ☐ **a.** have low operating costs.
   - ☐ **b.** can buy large orders at a discount.
   - ☐ **c.** provide better service.

3. If Claire and her team are wrong and people will not buy the purses for $15.99,
   - ☐ **a.** Top-Mart may lose $71,250.
   - ☐ **b.** the purses will probably go on sale.
   - ☐ **c.** Top-Mart will try to sell each purse for the unit price of $10.

4. Because the final markup was higher than the first markup,
   - ☐ **a.** customers may complain about the retail price.
   - ☐ **b.** the supplier will probably raise its unit price for purses.
   - ☐ **c.** Top-Mart can still make a profit if the purses go on sale.

5. Records of sales from earlier years probably help buyers such as Claire to
   - ☐ **a.** set retail prices.
   - ☐ **b.** decide what amounts to order.
   - ☐ **c.** estimate operating costs.

C. Reading Strategies

1. Recognizing Words in Context

Find the word *considers* in the article. One definition below is closest to the meaning of that word. One definition has the opposite or nearly the opposite meaning. The remaining definition has a meaning that has nothing to do with the word. Label the definitions **C** for *closest*, **O** for *opposite* or *nearly opposite*, and **U** for *unrelated*.

_____ **a.** ignores

_____ **b.** thinks of

_____ **c.** writes about

2. Distinguishing Fact from Opinion

Two of the statements below present *facts*, which can be proved. The other statement is an *opinion*, which expresses someone's thoughts or beliefs. Label the statements **F** for *fact* and **O** for *opinion*.

_____ **a.** Stores add markups to their prices in order to make money.

_____ **b.** Some suppliers give discounts to stores who buy large quantities of items.

_____ **c.** Customers should not buy an item until a store offers a discount on it.

3. Making Correct Inferences

Two of the statements below are correct *inferences*, or reasonable guesses, that are based on information in the article. The other statement is an incorrect, or faulty, inference. Label the statements **C** for *correct* inference and **I** for *incorrect* inference.

_____ **a.** When stores add a profit markup to prices, they always make a profit.

_____ **b.** A high price on an item may cause some customers not to buy it.

_____ **c.** If many customers want to buy an item, the store is likely to add a higher markup.

4. Understanding Main Ideas

One of the statements below expresses the main idea of the article. Another statement is too general, or too broad. The other explains only part of the article; it is too narrow. Label the statements **M** for *main idea*, **B** for *too broad*, and **N** for *too narrow*.

_____ **a.** Stores must consider operating costs when they decide on prices for their items.

_____ **b.** Buyers use discounts and markups to set prices that will help their store make a profit.

_____ **c.** Stores consider many things before they set prices for their goods.

5. Responding to the Article

Complete the following sentence in your own words:

Reading "Discounts and Markups Make a Profit" made me want to learn more about

_____

because _____

_____

D. Expanding Vocabulary

Content-Area Words

Complete each sentence with a word from the box. Write the missing word on the line.

trends	unit price	quantity	discount	markup

1. Lily bought a few shirts of high quality rather than a large _____ of cheap shirts.

2. After a 60-percent _____, the price of the book will be $16.

3. Danilo likes to be different and to ignore current _____.

4. Twelve candy bars in a box that costs $6 have a _____ of $0.50 per bar.

5. When a store lowers the price of an item, the customer gets a _____.

Academic English

In the article "Discounts and Markups Make a Profit," you learned that *style* means "a particular type of fashion." *Style* can also mean "a way of doing something that sets one apart from others," as in the following sentence.

Mr. Roumain speaks in a very formal style and makes almost no jokes.

Complete the sentence below.

1. Marla's *style* of painting is interesting because _____

Now use the word *style* in a sentence of your own.

2. _____

_____

You also learned that *contribute* means "to help to bring about a specific result." *Contribute* can also mean "to give something along with others for a common purpose," as in the following sentence.

Many people contribute money to groups that help people in need.

Complete the sentence below.

3. One way to *contribute* to a discussion is to _____

Now use the word *contribute* in two sentences of your own.

4. _____

5. _____

 Share your new sentences with a partner.

Before You Read

 Think about what you know. Read the lesson title above. What do you think the article will be about? Have you ever watched or played baseball?

Vocabulary

The content-area and academic English words below appear in "Pitching Baseball's Numbers." Read the definitions and the example sentences.

Content-Area Words

offense (ô′fens) the team or players that have the ball or puck and may score
> *Example:* The team that has the basketball is on *offense*.

defense (dē′fens) the team or players that try to stop the other team from scoring
> *Example:* We lost the game because our *defense* was weak.

decimal (des′ə məl) a fraction formed by dividing a number by ten or a power of ten, expressed as numbers after a period
> *Example:* The fraction ¼ written as a *decimal* is .25.

batting average (bat′ing av′rij) a ratio that compares the number of hits a baseball player gets to the number of times he or she has batted
> *Example:* The coach wanted to add a new player with a high *batting average*.

fielding percentage (fēl′ding pər sen′tij) a statistic that shows how well a baseball player throws and catches in the field
> *Example:* The baseball player with bad aim had a low *fielding percentage*.

Academic English

assist (ə sist′) an action in a sport that helps a teammate to score
> *Example:* Carlos got an *assist* when he threw the basketball to Marco, who scored.

errors (er′ərz) the failures of baseball players in the field to make plays that would put a runner or a batter out
> *Example:* The two *errors* that Jesse made resulted in a loss for his team.

Do any of the words above seem related? Sort the seven vocabulary words into two or more categories. Write the words down on note cards or in a chart. Words may fit into more than one group. You may wish to work with a partner for this activity. Label one category *Baseball Positions*.

 Now skim the article and look for other words that are new to you. Write each new word and its definition in the Personal Dictionary.

While You Read

Tip! **Think about why you read.** Do you think it is better for a baseball player's statistics to be high or low? As you read, look for one baseball statistic that is better when it is low.

Pitching Baseball's Numbers

1 Baseball statistics provide information about how well players and teams are playing in a season. Some baseball statistics simply involve counting things, such as when people add together the number of hits by a player. Other statistics are percentages. Player statistics give information about three types of player

5 performance: **offense, defense,** and pitching.

A batting "average" in baseball is not really an average. It is a ratio that people show as a **decimal.** The **batting average** shows how often a player gets a hit. To calculate the batting average, people divide the number of hits a player gets by the total number of at-bats, or times a player bats. If a player bats 120 times and

10 gets 30 hits, the batting average is .250 (30 ÷ 120 = .250). A high batting average, such as .390, shows that the player is a very good batter. A player with a .390 average gets a hit almost 4 out of 10 times at bat, on average.

The **fielding percentage** is a defense statistic that shows how well a player fields, or plays out in the field. If a player catches a fly ball, the batter is out. This

15 is called a *putout.* If a player gets a ground ball and throws it to the first baseman, the first baseman may be able to tag the runner out. This is an **assist** for the fielder and a putout for the first baseman. To calculate fielding percentage, people add together the player's assists and putouts and divide that number by the player's assists and putouts plus **errors.** A player who has 172 putouts, 3 assists,

20 and 1 error has a fielding percentage of .994 (175 ÷ 176 = .994).

A common pitching statistic is the earned run average (ERA). An earned run is a run that is scored because the pitcher let a batter get a hit. The ERA is the average number of earned runs that a pitcher gives up, or allows, in a normal nine-inning game. To calculate the ERA of a pitcher, people look at the total

25 number of earned runs the pitcher allowed. They multiply the earned runs by nine. Then they divide that number by the total number of innings that the player pitched. If a pitcher allows 35 earned runs in 70 innings, the ERA is 4.50 (35 × 9 = 315; 315 ÷ 70 = 4.50). A good ERA is 3.00 or less.

To calculate the winning percentage of a team, people divide the total number

30 of games won by the total number of games played. A team that has played 93 games and won 49 of them has a winning percentage of .527. This means that the team has won more than half of its games.

CONTENT CONNECTION

The All-American Girls Professional Baseball League began in 1943. A player named Joanne Weaver had the best batting average in the League. She averaged .429 in the League's last season in 1954. What sports do you like to watch? Do you pay attention to the players' or teams' statistics?

LANGUAGE CONNECTION

The letters *ERA* are an abbreviation for *earned run average.* An abbreviation is one or more letters that represent a whole word or phrase. What does the abbreviation *USA* stand for?

After You Read

A. Organizing Ideas

What can you learn from baseball statistics? Complete the chart below. In the second column, write down the information you would need to know to calculate each statistic. In the third column, write down what you can learn from each statistic. Refer to the article for information. The first row has been done for you.

Baseball Statistic	Information I Need to Know to Calculate It	What It Tells Me About a Player or Team
batting average	number of hits a player gets; number of times a player bats	I learn how good a player is at bat from the percentage of times he or she gets a hit.
fielding percentage		
earned run average		
winning percentage		

What did you learn about baseball statistics? Write two or more sentences to answer this question. Did the chart help you understand the different statistics? How?

_____

_____

_____

B. Comprehension Skills

Tip! **Think about how to find answers.** Look back at different parts of the text. What facts help you figure out how to complete the sentences?

Mark box **a, b,** or **c** with an **X** before the choice that best completes each sentence.

Recalling Facts

1. Baseball statistics give information about offense, defense, and
   - ☐ **a.** batting.
   - ☐ **b.** statistics.
   - ☐ **c.** pitching.

2. The number of hits a batter gets divided by the total number of at-bats is the
   - ☐ **a.** putout average.
   - ☐ **b.** batting average.
   - ☐ **c.** fielding percentage.

3. Defense statistics in baseball provide information about how well a player
   - ☐ **a.** bats.
   - ☐ **b.** fields.
   - ☐ **c.** pitches.

4. A batter with a batting average of .390
   - ☐ **a.** has been at bat 390 times.
   - ☐ **b.** gets a hit almost every time at bat.
   - ☐ **c.** gets about 4 hits for every 10 times at bat.

5. To calculate a team's winning percentage, divide the number of wins by
   - ☐ **a.** the number of losses.
   - ☐ **b.** the number of games played.
   - ☐ **c.** the number of tie games.

Understanding Ideas

1. A pitcher with an ERA of 2.60
   - ☐ **a.** is better than most pitchers.
   - ☐ **b.** gives up less than three runs in every game.
   - ☐ **c.** gives up almost three runs in every inning.

2. If a pitcher begins to allow more home runs,
   - ☐ **a.** the pitcher will become a batter.
   - ☐ **b.** the pitcher's ERA will go up.
   - ☐ **c.** the pitcher's ERA will go down.

3. A player with a high fielding percentage
   - ☐ **a.** has more assists than putouts.
   - ☐ **b.** has made many assists in the field.
   - ☐ **c.** has made few errors in the field.

4. If a team finishes the season with a winning percentage over .500, it
   - ☐ **a.** won more games than it lost.
   - ☐ **b.** lost more games than it won.
   - ☐ **c.** lost as many games as it won.

5. From the article, you can conclude that baseball statistics do not show
   - ☐ **a.** how well a player is playing.
   - ☐ **b.** how hard a team is trying to win.
   - ☐ **c.** how teams compare to one another.

C. Reading Strategies

1. Recognizing Words in Context

Find the word *performance* in the article. One definition below is closest to the meaning of that word. One definition has the opposite or nearly the opposite meaning. The remaining definition has a meaning that has nothing to do with the word. Label the definitions **C** for *closest,* **O** for *opposite* or *nearly opposite,* and **U** for *unrelated.*

_____ **a.** how well a person does a job

_____ **b.** when a person has no job

_____ **c.** how much a person likes a job

2. Distinguishing Fact from Opinion

Two of the statements below present *facts,* which can be proved. The other statement is an *opinion,* which expresses someone's thoughts or beliefs. Label the statements **F** for *fact* and **O** for *opinion.*

_____ **a.** For a pitcher, a low ERA is better than a high ERA.

_____ **b.** Batting average is the most important player statistic in baseball.

_____ **c.** Errors are bad for the fielding percentage of a player.

3. Making Correct Inferences

Two of the statements below are correct *inferences,* or reasonable guesses, that are based on information in the article. The other statement is an incorrect, or faulty, inference. Label the statements **C** for *correct* inference and **I** for *incorrect* inference.

_____ **a.** In baseball, the defense tries to keep the other team from scoring runs.

_____ **b.** A putout may or may not involve an assist from another player.

_____ **c.** If a player has a low batting average, he or she is not helping the team in any way.

4. Understanding Main Ideas

One of the statements below expresses the main idea of the article. Another statement is too general, or too broad. The other explains only part of the article; it is too narrow. Label the statements **M** for *main idea,* **B** for *too broad,* and **N** for *too narrow.*

_____ **a.** Batting average is a statistic that shows how often a player gets a hit.

_____ **b.** Baseball statistics show both player and team performance in offense, defense, and pitching.

_____ **c.** Sports often use statistics to measure player performance.

5. Responding to the Article

Complete the following sentence in your own words:

From reading "Pitching Baseball's Numbers," I have learned

_____

_____

D. Expanding Vocabulary

Content-Area Words

Read each item carefully. Write on the line the word or phrase that best completes each sentence.

1. A baseball player with _____ has a high fielding percentage.

   few errors   many errors   no putouts

2. Baseball players do not _____ when their team is on defense.

   catch   throw   bat

3. On the math test, we had to write each answer as either a _____ or a decimal.

   number   fraction   formula

4. When a baseball team is on offense, it tries to _____.

   make putouts   score runs   get assists

5. A batting average of .190 is _____.

   high   low   average

Academic English

In the article "Pitching Baseball's Numbers," you learned that *assist* is a noun that means "an action in a sport that helps a teammate to score." *Assist* can also be a verb that means "to help," as in the following sentence.

   The teacher will assist students who need help with their projects.

Complete the sentence below.

1. Police officers may *assist* drivers when _____

Now use the word *assist* in a sentence of your own.

2. _____

   _____

You also learned that *errors* means "the failures of baseball players in the field to make plays that would put a runner or a batter out." *Errors* can also mean "mistakes," as in the following sentence.

   Errors in math calculations will lead to incorrect answers.

Complete the sentence below.

3. To avoid *errors* in spelling, people may check a _____

Now use the word *errors* in two sentences of your own.

4. _____

5. _____

 Share your new sentences with a partner.

Before You Read

 Think about what you know. Skim the article on the opposite page. What do you know about beats in music? How do musicians know how long each note should be?

Vocabulary

The content-area and academic English words below appear in "How to Count Music in 4/4 Time." Read the definitions and the example sentences.

Content-Area Words

beat (bēt) the rhythm of music
 Example: I like to tap my feet to the *beat* of my favorite song.

measures (mezh′ərz) equal groups of beats in a piece of music
 Example: In 4/4 time, each of the *measures* has four beats.

meter (mē′tər) the number and length of beats in a measure of music
 Example: Some songs change *meter* between sections of the song.

time signature (tīm sig′nə chər) a symbol that shows a song's meter with two numbers that look similar to a fraction
 Example: One common *time signature* is 4/4; another is 3/4.

note (nōt) a musical tone, or the symbol that shows it on a piece of sheet music
 Example: The trumpet player held a long *note* at the end of the song.

Academic English

indicates (in′di kāts′) shows
 Example: An arrow *indicates* direction when it points toward something.

equivalent (i kwiv′ə lənt) equal in amount or value
 Example: A dime is *equivalent* to two nickels.

Read again the example sentences that follow the content-area and academic English word definitions. With a partner, discuss the meanings of the words and sentences. Then make up a sentence of your own for each word.

 Now skim the article and look for other words that are new to you. Write each new word and its definition in the Personal Dictionary.

While You Read

Tip! **Think about why you read.** Do you think math can help you play music? What ideas from math are used in music? As you read, look for ways that fractions and addition are related to music.

How to Count Music in 4/4 Time

LANGUAGE CONNECTION

Beat in line 1 is used as a noun. *Beat* can also be a verb that means "to win against." Try to use the word *beat* as a verb in a sentence.

1 Every song has a **beat.** The beat is what people tap their feet to when they listen to music. **Measures** are groups of beats. Each measure has the same number of beats. The number and length of beats in a measure make up the **meter** of the song. When people write music down, they show the meter of a 5 song with a symbol called the *time signature.* On sheet music, the time signature looks like a fraction without a line to separate the top and bottom numbers. One of the most common musical time signatures is 4/4 meter.

The time signature of a song tells people two things. First, it shows the number of beats in each measure. Second, it **indicates** what kind of **note** gets 10 one full beat. In 4/4 meter, the top 4 means that each measure has four beats. The bottom 4 means that a quarter note gets one full beat.

There are many different kinds of musical notes. Note length is the amount of time that a musician should hold the note. People measure note lengths in fractions. There are whole notes, half notes, quarter notes, eighth notes, 15 sixteenth notes, thirty-second notes, sixty-fourth notes, and so on. People add together note lengths to fill all of the beats in a measure. In 4/4 meter, a quarter note is one beat long, and each measure has four beats. The lengths of the other notes are based on the length of the quarter note. In 4/4 meter, a sixteenth note is a quarter of a beat, and an eighth note is half of a beat. A half note is two beats, 20 and a whole note lasts for four beats.

To fill one measure in 4/4 meter, you could use one whole note or two half notes. You could also use four quarter notes, eight eighth notes, or sixteen sixteenth notes. Or you could mix and match different types of notes, as long as the sum of the note lengths is **equivalent** to four beats. One measure may 25 contain two eighth notes, a half note, and a quarter note. Another measure may contain eight sixteenth notes, two eighth notes, and a quarter note. Think about the song "Old MacDonald Had a Farm." The first line, the title of the song, is made up of two measures. Each of the measures has four beats. The first measure has four quarter notes, and the second measure has two quarter notes 30 and one half note. Tap a pencil against a desk to try it!

CONTENT CONNECTION

If a sixteenth note is equal to a quarter of a beat, and an eighth note is equal to half of a beat, how many sixteenth notes are equal to one eighth note? How many sixteenth notes are equal to one quarter note?

After You Read

A. Applying the Math

Can you count music in 4/4 time? Complete the chart below. Imagine that each box is one measure in 4/4 meter. In each box, write down a group of notes with lengths that add up to four beats. Write down the length of each note. Use at least two or three different kinds of notes in each measure. Use the article to help you. One measure has been done for you.

Measure 1	Measure 2	Measure 3	Measure 4
	eighth note = ½ beat eighth note = ½ beat eighth note = ½ beat eighth note = ½ beat quarter note = 1 beat quarter note = 1 beat		
Total = 4 beats	**Total =** 4 beats	**Total =** 4 beats	**Total =** 4 beats

What did you learn about the different types of notes in 4/4 meter? Why do some measures have fewer notes than others do? Write two or more sentences to answer these questions. Did the chart help you understand 4/4 time better? Why or why not?

_____

_____

_____

_____

_____

_____

_____

_____

_____

B. Comprehension Skills

Tip! **Think about how to find answers.** Think about what each sentence means. Try to say it yourself in your own words before you complete it.

Mark box **a, b,** or **c** with an **X** before the choice that best completes each sentence.

Recalling Facts

1. The number and length of beats in a measure is the
   - ☐ **a.** meter of a song.
   - ☐ **b.** signature of a song.
   - ☐ **c.** tune of a song.

2. To find the meter of a song, look at
   - ☐ **a.** the measure.
   - ☐ **b.** a quarter note.
   - ☐ **c.** the time signature.

3. Each measure in a song has the same number of
   - ☐ **a.** beats.
   - ☐ **b.** meters.
   - ☐ **c.** time signatures.

4. In a 4/4 time signature, the top number 4 shows the number of
   - ☐ **a.** notes in each measure.
   - ☐ **b.** measures in the song.
   - ☐ **c.** beats in each measure.

5. In a 4/4 time signature, the bottom number 4 shows
   - ☐ **a.** what kind of note receives one beat.
   - ☐ **b.** the number of beats in each measure.
   - ☐ **c.** that a quarter note receives four beats.

Understanding Ideas

1. From the article, you can conclude that
   - ☐ **a.** all modern music uses 4/4 meter.
   - ☐ **b.** music is not written in 4/4 meter very often.
   - ☐ **c.** a great deal of music is written in 4/4 meter.

2. Two whole notes in 4/4 meter equal
   - ☐ **a.** two beats.
   - ☐ **b.** four beats.
   - ☐ **c.** eight beats.

3. In music with the time signature 3/4, each measure has
   - ☐ **a.** four beats.
   - ☐ **b.** three beats.
   - ☐ **c.** seven beats.

4. A time signature of 2/4 means that
   - ☐ **a.** the music is played twice as fast as 4/4 meter.
   - ☐ **b.** each measure has two beats and a quarter note gets one beat.
   - ☐ **c.** the music contains only half notes and quarter notes.

5. From the article, you can conclude that
   - ☐ **a.** the time signature helps musicians know how to play a piece of music.
   - ☐ **b.** 4/4 meter is the best meter for children's songs.
   - ☐ **c.** only songs in 4/4 meter have a regular beat.

C. Reading Strategies

1. Recognizing Words in Context

Find the word *separate* in the article. One definition below is closest to the meaning of that word. One definition has the opposite or nearly the opposite meaning. The remaining definition has a meaning that has nothing to do with the word. Label the definitions **C** for *closest*, **O** for *opposite* or *nearly opposite*, and **U** for *unrelated*.

_____ **a.** draw

_____ **b.** put together

_____ **c.** divide

2. Distinguishing Fact from Opinion

Two of the statements below present *facts*, which can be proved. The other statement is an *opinion*, which expresses someone's thoughts or beliefs. Label the statements **F** for *fact* and **O** for *opinion*.

_____ **a.** In 4/4 meter, a whole note takes up an entire measure.

_____ **b.** Each measure in 4/4 meter contains a group of notes that equals four beats.

_____ **c.** Music in 4/4 meter is the best kind to dance to.

3. Making Correct Inferences

Two of the statements below are correct *inferences*, or reasonable guesses, that are based on information in the article. The other statement is an incorrect, or faulty, inference. Label the statements **C** for *correct* inference and **I** for *incorrect* inference.

_____ **a.** Musicians know how to read music symbols such as notes and time signatures.

_____ **b.** Whenever people learn about music, they learn about 4/4 meter first.

_____ **c.** In some meters, a quarter note does not get one beat.

4. Understanding Main Ideas

One of the statements below expresses the main idea of the article. Another statement is too general, or too broad. The other explains only part of the article; it is too narrow. Label the statements **M** for *main idea*, **B** for *too broad*, and **N** for *too narrow*.

_____ **a.** In 4/4 meter, each measure has four beats, and a quarter note gets one beat.

_____ **b.** On sheet music, the time signature shows the meter of a song.

_____ **c.** One common musical time signature is 4/4 meter.

5. Responding to the Article

Complete the following sentence in your own words:

One thing in "How to Count Music in 4/4 Time" that I cannot understand is

_____

_____

D. Expanding Vocabulary

Content-Area Words

Cross out one word in each row that is not related to the word in dark type.

1. beat	rhythm	music	meter	tone
2. measures	beats	groups	music	signature
3. meter	beats	ruler	length	measure
4. time signature	meter	fraction	author	numbers
5. note	practice	symbol	music	length

Academic English

In the article "How to Count Music in 4/4 Time," you learned that *indicates* means "shows." *Indicates* can also mean "is a sign of," as in the following sentence.

A dark, cloudy sky indicates that it is going to rain.

Complete the sentence below.

1. A yawn *indicates* that a person is _____

Now use the word *indicates* in a sentence of your own.

2. _____

_____

You also learned that *equivalent* means "equal in amount or value." *Equivalent* can refer to different groups of notes that equal four beats. *Equivalent* can also refer to other things that are equal in amount or value, as in the following sentence.

One year is equivalent in time to 365 days.

Complete the sentence below.

3. Twelve inches are *equivalent* to one _____

Now use the word *equivalent* in two sentences of your own.

4. _____

5. _____

 Share your new sentences with a partner.

Time to Paint the House

Before You Read

Tip! **Think about what you know.** Read the title and the first paragraph of the article on the opposite page. What do you think the article will be about? Have you ever painted a room, a piece of furniture, or something else that is part of your home?

Vocabulary

The content-area and academic English words below appear in "Time to Paint the House." Read the definitions and the example sentences.

Content-Area Words

container (kən tā′nər) an object that can hold other items
Example: Juice often comes in a plastic *container* from the grocery store.

square feet (skwār fēt) units used to measure surface area in one-foot squares
Example: This bedroom floor will need 150 *square feet* of carpet.

gallon (gal′ən) a unit used to measure how much liquid something holds
Example: Harmony bought a *gallon* of milk on sale for $1.99.

surface area (sur′fis ār′ē ə) the amount of surface, or outer face, that something has
Example: Our living room has a larger *surface area* than my bedroom does.

quart (kwôrt) a unit used to measure how much liquid something holds; equal to one-fourth of a gallon
Example: I drink a *quart* of bottled water every day.

Academic English

task (task) a job or piece of work to be done
Example: My *task* is to wash the dishes after our family dinner.

sufficient (sə fish′ənt) necessary; enough
Example: Trees will die without *sufficient* water and sunlight.

Rate each vocabulary word according to the following scale. Write a number next to each content-area and academic English word.

4   I have never seen the word before.

3   I have seen the word but do not know what it means.

2   I know what the word means when I read it.

1   I use the word myself in speaking or writing.

Dictionary Now skim the article and look for other words that are new to you. Write each new word and its definition in the Personal Dictionary.

While You Read

Tip! **Think about why you read.** If you have to paint a room, how do you decide how much paint to buy? What information helps you decide? As you read, look for the information that helps you calculate the amount of paint to buy.

Time to PAINT THE HOUSE

1 Every house needs a fresh coat of paint from time to time. After painters know which color to use, they must figure out how much paint they need for the **task.** They use math to make this calculation.

The label of each paint **container** states how many **square feet** the paint will
5 cover. A **gallon** is usually enough for 400 to 450 square feet of **surface area.** The surface area is the amount of wall and ceiling space that needs new paint. People measure surface area in square feet. Painters need to find out how many square feet of wall and ceiling space need paint.

Imagine that you need to figure out the total surface area for the walls and
10 ceiling of a bedroom that is 10 feet by 12 feet. The walls in the room are 8 feet high. The room has a window that is 3 feet by 4 feet and a door that is 3 feet by 7 feet. What is the total surface area that needs paint? Two walls of the bedroom are each 10 feet long and 8 feet high. Eight feet times 10 feet equals 80 square feet for each of the two walls. The other two walls are each 12 feet long and 8
15 feet high. They are 96 square feet each. The ceiling is 10 feet by 12 feet, or 120 square feet. When you add together the surface areas of the four walls and the ceiling, you find that the total is 472 square feet.

Next subtract the areas that do not need paint: the window and the door. You can figure out the areas of the window and the door in the same way that you
20 figured out the areas of the walls and the ceiling. The area of the window is 12 square feet. The area of the door is 21 square feet. This means that you must subtract a total of 33 square feet from the 472 square feet. You find that 439 square feet is the total surface area that needs paint. Because a single gallon of paint will cover 450 square feet, you need to buy only one gallon of paint for
25 the bedroom.

What if you want to use a **quart** of a different color of paint for the ceiling? Will a quart be a **sufficient** amount of paint? A quart is one-fourth of a gallon. If a gallon will cover 400 to 450 square feet, a quart will cover 100 to 112.5 square feet. The ceiling is 120 square feet, so a quart of paint will not be enough.

LANGUAGE CONNECTION

The phrase *from time to time* is an idiom that means "occasionally" or "once in a while." An idiom is a phrase with a meaning that cannot be figured out from the definitions of each word. Restate the first sentence of the article in your own words.

CONTENT CONNECTION

The White House, the home of the U.S. president, has 132 rooms and 35 bathrooms. It also has 412 doors, 147 windows, 8 staircases, and 3 elevators. How many gallons of paint would you guess that it takes to cover the outside of the White House?

After You Read

A. Applying the Math

How much of the surface area in a room needs paint? Imagine that you need to paint the walls of a bedroom. The sizes of the walls, windows, and door are listed below. Draw each of the four walls, including the windows and the door. Label the lengths in feet. Then color in the areas that need paint. One wall has been started for you.

Room Measurements

Two walls: 12 feet long by 8 feet high
Two windows: 3 feet by 3 feet
One door: 3 feet wide by 7 feet high

Two walls: 10 feet long by 8 feet high
Three windows: 2 feet wide by 3 feet high

window | 3 feet

3 feet

8 feet

12 feet

How do you calculate the amount of surface area that needs paint? Write two or more sentences to answer this question. Did this activity help you understand the article? How?

_____

_____

_____

B. Comprehension Skills

Tip! **Think about how to find answers.** Look back at what you read. The information is in the text, but you may have to look in several sentences to find it.

Mark box **a, b,** or **c** with an **X** before the choice that best completes each sentence.

Recalling Facts

1. The amount of wall or ceiling space that needs new paint is the
   - ☐ **a.** upper limit.
   - ☐ **b.** surface area.
   - ☐ **c.** feet-to-surface ratio.

2. To find out how many square feet a container of paint will cover, look
   - ☐ **a.** on the shelf in the store.
   - ☐ **b.** in books and magazines.
   - ☐ **c.** at the label of the container.

3. A gallon of paint will usually cover
   - ☐ **a.** 300 to 350 square feet.
   - ☐ **b.** 400 to 450 square feet.
   - ☐ **c.** 500 to 600 square feet.

4. Before painters buy paint, they
   - ☐ **a.** clean the floor of the room.
   - ☐ **b.** sand the walls with sandpaper.
   - ☐ **c.** figure out the total surface area that needs paint.

5. After you figure out the areas of the surfaces that do not need paint, you must
   - ☐ **a.** ignore them.
   - ☐ **b.** add them to the total surface area.
   - ☐ **c.** subtract them from the total surface area.

Understanding Ideas

1. To find the total surface area that needs paint in a room,
   - ☐ **a.** multiply the surface areas of the four walls.
   - ☐ **b.** add together the surface areas that need paint.
   - ☐ **c.** find the surface area of one wall and multiply it by four.

2. The surface area of a ceiling that is 10 feet by 13 feet is
   - ☐ **a.** 100 square feet.
   - ☐ **b.** 130 square feet.
   - ☐ **c.** 300 square feet.

3. A quart of paint will cover about
   - ☐ **a.** 100 square feet.
   - ☐ **b.** 300 square feet.
   - ☐ **c.** 400 square feet.

4. From the article, you can conclude that
   - ☐ **a.** a gallon of paint is usually enough to paint a small bedroom.
   - ☐ **b.** painters must know how to divide to calculate surface areas.
   - ☐ **c.** all painters use the same method to figure out how much paint to buy.

5. You can also conclude that
   - ☐ **a.** a gallon of paint will cover 600 square feet.
   - ☐ **b.** a ceiling is not part of the surface area of a room.
   - ☐ **c.** a room with many windows needs less paint than a room of the same size with no windows.

C. Reading Strategies

1. Recognizing Words in Context

Find the word *fresh* in the article. One definition below is closest to the meaning of that word. One definition has the opposite or nearly the opposite meaning. The remaining definition has a meaning that has nothing to do with the word. Label the definitions **C** for *closest*, **O** for *opposite* or *nearly opposite*, and **U** for *unrelated*.

_____ **a.** new

_____ **b.** old

_____ **c.** empty

2. Distinguishing Fact from Opinion

Two of the statements below present *facts*, which can be proved. The other statement is an *opinion*, which expresses someone's thoughts or beliefs. Label the statements **F** for *fact* and **O** for *opinion*.

_____ **a.** A quart is smaller than a gallon.

_____ **b.** People measure surface area in square feet.

_____ **c.** Painters should purchase more paint than they think they need.

3. Making Correct Inferences

Two of the statements below are correct *inferences*, or reasonable guesses, that are based on information in the article. The other statement is an incorrect, or faulty, inference. Label the statements **C** for *correct* inference and **I** for *incorrect* inference.

_____ **a.** A room with many large windows is likely to have a small surface area to paint.

_____ **b.** A gallon of paint will always be enough to cover 450 square feet.

_____ **c.** People usually buy paint in gallon and quart amounts.

4. Understanding Main Ideas

One of the statements below expresses the main idea of the article. Another statement is too general, or too broad. The other explains only part of the article; it is too narrow. Label the statements **M** for *main idea*, **B** for *too broad*, and **N** for *too narrow*.

_____ **a.** Painters measure a room before they paint it.

_____ **b.** To figure out the amount of paint they need, painters calculate the surface area of the room and subtract the areas that do not need paint.

_____ **c.** A square foot is the unit that people commonly use to measure surface area.

5. Responding to the Article

Complete the following sentences in your own words:

One of the things I did best while reading "Time to Paint the House" was

_____

I think that I did this well because _____

_____

D. Expanding Vocabulary

Content-Area Words

Complete each sentence with a word from the box. Write the missing word on the line.

container	square feet	gallon	surface area	quart

1. A floor that measures 10 feet by 10 feet is 100 _____.

2. A tin can is a type of _____.

3. To paint a small closet, Hattori needs only a _____ of paint.

4. Do we have enough paint to cover the _____ of this room?

5. My mom's car travels 20 miles on each _____ of gasoline.

Academic English

In the article "Time to Paint the House," you learned that *task* means "a job or piece of work to be done." *Task* can also mean "a tiring or boring job or duty," as in the following sentence.

   My least favorite task is making my bed.

Complete the sentence below.

1. No one wanted the *task* of _____

Now use the word *task* in a sentence of your own.

2. _____

_____

You also learned that *sufficient* means "necessary" or "enough." *Sufficient* can describe the amount of paint that is enough to cover the walls of a room. *Sufficient* can also describe other amounts that are necessary or enough, as in the following sentence.

   Ernesto will be late if he does not allow sufficient travel time.

Complete the sentence below.

3. When Anuja does not get *sufficient* sleep, she is _____

Now use the word *sufficient* in two sentences of your own.

4. _____

5. _____

 Share your new sentences with a partner.

Writing a Newspaper Advertisement

Read the advertisement. Then complete the sentences. Use words from the Word Bank.

Music Classes at Rhythm Music School

Word Bank

beat   indicates

assist   accommodate

styles

Do you tap your foot to the (1) _____ of music? This (2) _____ that you may have a hidden musical talent. Come explore different instruments and different (3) _____ of music at Rhythm Music School. Our teachers will (4) _____ you as you learn to read notes and understand meter. Sign up for Music Exploration Night—but hurry, because we can only (5) _____ 50 students. Call now, and soon you could be an expert musician!

Sign up now!

Reading an Instant-Messaging Conversation

Read the instant-messaging conversation between Kia and Tang. Circle the word that completes each sentence.

INSTA-CHAT

Kia: Hi, Tang! I'm excited for the soccer season to start! I want to play (**offense, defense**) this year so that I can try to score goals.

Tang: I'm excited, too. Do you want to shop for new soccer shoes tonight? City Sports Store gives students a (**quart, discount**).

Kia: Should we go to Soccer Supply Store, too?

Tang: Their shoes are nice, but they are too expensive for me. Maybe Coach Barr could order them in a large (**quantity, container**) for the whole team. Then the price may be lower.

Kia: That's a great idea! I'm sure Coach Barr wants to (**markup, ensure**) that we all have good shoes.

Tang: If we talk to her tomorrow, Coach Barr will have (**sufficient, decimal**) time to order shoes before the first game.

Kia: Let's do it! I hope she says yes.

 **Making Connections**

Work with a partner. Talk about what the words mean. How have you heard people use these words? List your ideas in the chart below.

meter	note	unit	measurement	surface area
contribute	culture	task	equivalent	errors

Word	How I Have Heard People Use It

Use all of the words above in complete sentences of your own. Each sentence may include one or more of the words. To help you start writing, look at the ideas you wrote about. After you write your sentences, read them over. If you find a mistake, correct it.

_____

_____

_____

_____

_____

_____

Glossary

A

accommodate (ə kom′ə dāt′) to have enough room for a certain number of people or things [11]

***accurately** (ak′yər it lē) correctly [8]

addition (ə dish′ən) the process used to add numbers into one amount [7]

***adjust** (ə just′) to change something in order to achieve a goal [8]

advertising (ad′vər tī′zing) information about a product that is given to the public [10]

***allocated** (al′ə kāt′əd) set aside or gave for a certain purpose [4]

analysis (ə nal′ə sis) a careful, detailed study of something [9]

***annual** (an′ū əl) measured by the year [2]

***assist** (ə sist′) an action in a sport that helps a teammate to score [13]

athletes (ath′lēts) people who train for sports and other physical competitions [1]

average (av′rij) the sum of a set of numbers divided by how many numbers are in the set [9]

B

batting average (bat′ing av′rij) a ratio that compares the number of hits a baseball player gets to the number of times he or she has batted [13]

beat (bēt) the rhythm of music [14]

budget (buj′it) a plan to use a certain amount of money for a set purpose [3]

C

calculations (kal′kyə lā′shənz) mathematical steps taken to find an answer [7]

candidate (kan′də dit) a person who seeks to be elected to a certain office or position [4]

***category** (kat′ə gôr′ē) a group of things within a larger system [3]

charge (chärj) to ask as the price of a service or product [10]

circulation (sur′kyə lā′shən) the total number of copies that a newspaper sells each day [10]

combination (kom′bə nā′shen) a mixture; something formed by putting things together [6]

***comprise** (kəm prīz′) to include; to be made of [6]

***constant** (kon′stənt) not changing [9]

container (kən tā′nər) an object that can hold other items [15]

***contrast** (kon′trast) a difference between two things [1]

***contribute** (kən trib′ūt) to help to bring about a specific result [12]

***culture** (kul′chər) the arts, beliefs, and customs of a certain group of people [11]

D

daylight saving time (dā′līt′ sā′ving tīm) a period of time in which clocks are set one hour ahead to provide extra daylight during common work hours [8]

decimal (des′ə məl) a fraction formed by dividing a number by ten or a power of ten, expressed as numbers after a period [13]

deductions (di duk′shənz) amounts taken away or subtracted from a total [2]

D (continued)

defense (dē′fens) the team or players that try to stop the other team from scoring [13]

detail (dē′tāl) small parts or features of an item [6]

discount (dis′kount′) an amount that is subtracted from a full price [12]

E

earnings (ur′ningz) the money a person receives in exchange for work or services [1]

election (i lek′shən) an event at which people vote to choose a person for a position [4]

engineers (en′ji nērz′) people who design and build structures or machines [9]

***ensure** (en shoor′) to make sure or certain of something [11]

***equivalent** (i kwiv′ə lənt) equal in amount or value [14]

***errors** (er′ərz) the failures of baseball players in the field to make plays that would put a runner or a batter out [13]

***estimate** (es′tə māt′) to make an inexact or rough calculation of something [7]

ethnic (eth′nik) relating to a group of people who share a culture, race, or history [5]

***expand** (iks pand′) to make larger in size or amount [10]

expenses (iks pens′əz) items or services that people must spend money on [3]

F

***federal** (fed′ər əl) relating to the central government of the United States [2]

fielding percentage (fēl′ding pər sen′tij) a statistic that shows how well a baseball player throws and catches in the field [13]

formulas (fôr′myə ləz) mathematical ways to show a rule or solve a problem [9]

fortune (fôr′chən) the luck of a person, whether good or bad [11]

G

gallon (gal′ən) a unit used to measure how much liquid something holds [15]

gap (gap) a separation between two things [1]

generation (jen′ə rā′shən) a group of people that makes up one step in a family line [5]

geometric (jē′ə met′rik) made of lines, angles, and shapes such as circles and triangles [6]

grid (grid) a pattern made of many lines that cross to form squares [11]

gross (grōs) total [2]

I

*****immigrant** (im′ə grənt) a person who enters a new country and plans to stay there permanently [5]

income (in′kum′) money that a person receives as payment for work or services [2]

*****indicates** (in′di kāts′) shows [14]

industry (in′dəs trē) a branch of business, trade, or production [5]

insurance (in shoor′əns) protection against risk or loss; a contract that arranges for a person to pay money in exchange for a company's promise to pay money in the case of problems, such as illness or property damage [2]

J

*****justify** (jus′tə fī′) to show something to be a good decision [10]

L

longitude (lon′jə tood′) distance on Earth's surface, measured in degrees east and west [8]

M

manufactured (man′yə fak′chərd) made in large amounts, usually with the help of machines [6]

market (mär′kit) trade and the exchange of money for a certain service or product [1]

market share (mär′kit shār) the percentage of total sales that one company holds for a product or service [10]

markup (märk′up′) an amount that a seller adds to an item's price to make a profit [12]

measurement (mezh′ər mənt) the process of finding the exact size or amount of something [11]

measures (mezh′ərz) equal groups of beats in a piece of music [14]

meter (mē′tər) the number and length of beats in a measure of music [14]

*****minimum** (min′ə məm) the smallest necessary amount of something [4]

multiplication (mul′tə pli kā′shən) the process of adding a number to itself a certain number of times [7]

N

net (net) remaining after all deductions have been made [2]

note (nōt) a musical tone, or the symbol that shows it on a piece of sheet music [14]

O

offense (ô′fens) the team or players that have the ball or puck and may score [13]

P

percentage (pər sen′tij) a certain part of a whole expressed as parts out of every hundred [9]

population (pop′yə lā′shən) the number of people who live in a certain place [4]

*****predicted** (pri dikt′əd) used current knowledge to make a guess about the future [9]

prejudice (prej′ə dis) dislike of a group such as a race or religion [5]

prime meridian (prīm mə rid′ē ən) the zero-degree line of longitude, which all other lines of longitude are measured from [8]

*****process** (pros′es) a series of actions that lead to a certain result [7]

product (prod′əkt) the amount that is the result of multiplication [7]

---

* Academic English word

Lesson numbers appear in brackets.

production (prə duk′shən) the process of making something [3]

****professional** (prə fesh′ən əl) having a job that is the source of one's income or money [1]

profit (prof′it) the money that remains after a business has paid all of its costs [3]

Q

quantity (kwon′tə tē) the amount or number of something [12]

quart (kwôrt) a unit used to measure how much liquid something holds; equal to one-fourth of a gallon [15]

R

ratio (rā′shē ō′) a comparison in size or amount between two things [3]

representatives (rep′ri zen′tə tivz) elected members of the U.S. House of Representatives [4]

****require** (ri kwīr′) to have a need for something [6]

retail (rē′tāl) the sale of items in small amounts directly to the customer [5]

revenue (rev′ə nōō′) the amount of money that a company makes [10]

S

salary (sal′ə rē) a set amount of money that a person receives at regular times in exchange for work or services [1]

senators (sen′ə tərz) elected members of the U.S. Senate [4]

square feet (skwār fēt) units used to measure surface area in one-foot squares [15]

standardized (stan′dər dīzd′) caused things to use the same system [8]

****statistics** (stə tis′tiks) the collection and study of numbers that relate to certain subjects [5]

****style** (stīl) a particular type of fashion [12]

****sufficient** (sə fish′ənt) necessary; enough [15]

sum (sum) the amount that is the result of addition [7]

surface area (sur′fis ār′ē ə) the amount of surface, or outer face, that something has [15]

T

****task** (task) a job or piece of work to be done [15]

time signature (tīm sig′nə chər) a symbol that shows a song's meter with two numbers that look similar to a fraction [14]

trends (trendz) the general choices of a group of people at a certain time [12]

U

unit (ū′nit) a set amount of something used to measure other amounts of the same thing [11]

unit price (ū′nit prīs) the price for one item [12]

V

****vary** (vār′ē) to be different [3]

W

width (width) measurement from side to side [6]

Z

zones (zōnz) areas or regions that are different from nearby areas in some way [8]

---

* Academic English word

Lesson numbers appear in brackets.